Moodle 1.9
English Teacher's Cookbook

80 simple but incredibly effective recipes for teaching
reading comprehension, writing, and composing using
Moodle 1.9 and Web 2.0

Silvina P. Hillar

BIRMINGHAM - MUMBAI

Moodle 1.9 English Teacher's Cookbook

First published: June 2010

Production Reference: 1290610

Published by Packt Publishing Ltd.
32 Lincoln Road
Olton
Birmingham, B27 6PA, UK.

ISBN 978-1-849510-88-2

www.packtpub.com

Cover Image by Vinayak Chittar (vinayak.chittar@gmail.com)

Credits

Author
Silvina P. Hillar

Reviewer
Ben Reynolds

Acquisition Editor
Sarah Cullington

Development Editor
Swapna Verlekar

Technical Editor
Paramanand N. Bhat

Copy Editor
Lakshmi Menon

Indexer
Tejal Daruwale

Editorial Team Leader
Akshara Aware

Project Team Leader
Priya Mukherji

Project Coordinator
Zainab Bagasrawala

Proofreader
Kevin McGowan

Production Coordinator
Shantanu Zagade

Cover Work
Shantanu Zagade

About the Author

Silvina P. Hillar has been teaching English since 1993. She has always had a great interest in teaching, writing, and composing techniques, and has done a lot of research on this subject.

She is an English Teacher, a Certified Legal Translator (English/Spanish) and has a Post Degree in Education (graduated with Honors).

She has worked in several schools and institutes with native English speaking students. She has also worked as an independent consultant for many international companies essaying the role of an interpreter, translator, and e-learning activities developer.

She has always had a passion for educational technology. Formerly, videos and cassettes were a must in her teaching lessons; computer was and still is present. Her brother Gastón C. Hillar designed some programs and games for her courses. Lately, she is teaching using Moodle 1.9 and the Web 2.0. She believes that one of the most amazing challenges in education is bridging the gap between classic education and modern technologies.

She lives with her five-year-old son, Nico. When not tinkering with computers, she enjoys travelling to the seaside with her son, with whom she spends a lot of time at the beach.

You can reach her at silvinahillar@hotmail.com.

You can follow her on Twitter at: http://twitter.com/silvinahillar.

Acknowledgement

I would like to thank all the team at Packt Publishing Ltd., who worked with me as an incredibly helpful team. Sarah Cullington helped me to transform the original idea in the final book and to give my first steps working with a Cookbook. She was always ready to help and give good advice when I was doubtful. Zainab Bagasrawala guided me with patience through the process of writing. Swapna Verlekar also guided me in the development stage of the book and added wise comments to my original writings.

I would also like to thank Paramanand N. Bhat who has performed a great job as a Technical Editor, the reader will notice his work.

I wish to acknowledge my Reviewer, Ben Reynolds who has been very helpful with his comments and gave me good tips which I added to the different chapters. I must also thank my Proofreader Kevin McGowan for his thorough reviews.

I would also like to thank all my students, either real or virtual, who made it possible for me to be a teacher.

Special thanks to my five-year-old son, Nico, who despite his age was very patient and supporting in the writing process of the book, even though he does not want me to work at all! My parents, Susana and Jose (also a writer), who always stood by me and supported my decisions. My brother Gastón C. Hillar who helps me whenever I need him. My little one-year-old nephew Kevin and my sister in law Vanesa S. Olsen with whom we spend time working and exploring Moodle and Web 2.0 resources.

Many thanks to all my relatives, friends, and work colleagues who have helped me in different ways throughout the writing process of this book.

About the Reviewer

Ben Reynolds is a Senior Program Manager of CTYOnline at The Johns Hopkins University's Center for Talented Youth (CTY). An award-winning fictionist, he began CTY's face-to-face writing program in 1978 and launched CTYOnline's writing program in 1983. He began administrating CTYOnline's writing & language arts division in 1985. CTYOnline serves over 10,000 students a year in writing/language arts, math, science, computer science, Advanced Placement, and foreign languages. In the 1990's, Reynolds left the classroom for full-time administration both of CTY's writing/language arts program and of a residential site for CTY Summer Programs. Reynolds has also taught writing and the teaching of writing for the Johns Hopkins School of Continuing Studies. He holds a BA from Duke University, where he part-timed in the computer center, trading print out for punch cards, and an MA from Johns Hopkins in Fiction Writing. He is an active member of the Using Moodle community.

Dedicated to
To my son, Nico.

Table of Contents

Preface

This book begins with simple activities which enhance students' writing such as connecting activities developed in different ways either using Moodle or any other free and open source software available in the Web 2.0.

Next, it moves into matching images and different pieces of writing, it shows how to import different pictures to the Moodle course in different ways. It caters for a great variety of images which will enlighten the creativity of students.

Then, reading comprehension is explored from the characters' point of view. Students should explore reading in such a way as to become a part of it and write as if they were part of the story.

Twitter and Facebook social networks are embedded in the Moodle course so as to invent stories, create group works, and create social and popular interaction with the virtual classroom. There are step-by-step activities involving these websites, inserting Ishikawa's management technique in order to enhance group writing.

Once you have reached this point of the book, there are other writing techniques explored such as mathematical association to writing, cube technique, discussion clock, mind mapping, tree diagrams, among others. A step-by-step guide is provided for creating these techniques, uploading it into the Moodle course, and creating the writing activity.

The book covers writing sentences, poems, songs, descriptions, compositions, essays, articles, cartoons, Ads, creating superheroes and their descriptions.

This book was written with Moodle version 1.9.5 in mind. But the examples of this book are compatible with all the versions of Moodle 1.9 series.

What this book covers

Chapter 1, Connecting Ideas covers how to design several types of exercises so that students can enrich the use of connectors. Guided writing activities are also carried out such as answering a quiz, connecting stairs, writing a story out of pictures and completing a chart.

Chapter 2, Matching Pictures and Text covers how to work with reading comprehension, not only in the classical way, but also adding pictures so as to explore another side to it. After matching activities the writing part is a must.

Chapter 3, Looking at Things from Different Perspectives covers how to develop an interest in reading for our students. After reading comprehension activities, students are to write several pieces considering the fact that they are inside what they have already read.

Chapter 4, Defining Types of Sentences covers how to insert several types of activities concerning three types of sentences within a paragraph. The last recipe includes a structure on how to write a composition using the three types of sentences so as to do a coherent piece of writing.

Chapter 5, Creating Stories Using Twitter and Facebook covers how to embed both social networks in our Moodle course, and develop writing activities exploiting the resources of both of them. Apart from that we will use management technique and upload it into the social network.

Chapter 6, Improving Your Students' Writing covers cubing technique, showing how it works, exploring each side of the cube through interesting activities, after using all the sides of the cube in one recipe.

Chapter 7, Comparing Using Venn Diagram covers how to organize writing using Venn diagrams, which are drawn using different software, commercial and open source, and resources from the Web 2.0.

Chapter 8, Composing New Sceneries covers a wide range of colorful and interesting activities presenting students with well known items which they have to change or twist so as to create something different. Several resources from the Web 2.0 can be inserted in the Moodle course.

Chapter 9, Working with Mind Maps and Tree Diagrams covers how to design Mind Maps and Tree diagrams in different ways and upload or link them into our Moodle course. After that students create different pieces of writing.

Chapter 10, Preparing a Discussion Clock covers how to examine various viewpoints (12) after a given topic. Designing and uploading of different discussion clocks is covered in this chapter.

What you need for this book

Open source software, social networks, and commercial software.

Moodle, English grammar, Reading comprehension, writing, composing, connectors, Hot potatoes, Quandary 2, Web 2.0, embedding Twitter in Moodle, embedding Facebook in Moodle, Uploading images to Moodle, writing activities in Moodle, Venn diagrams in Moodle, Mind mapping in Moodle, embedding YouTube videos in Moodle, embedding TeacherTube in Moodle, creating cartoons, heroes, and tree diagrams in Moodle, and Ishikawa in Moodle. Basic experience with Moodle 1.9 or 1.9.5, as well as installation and configuration procedures is expected.

Who this book is for

If you are an English teacher who wants to find out practical, funny, and engaging activities to insert in your course, this is a perfectly designed book for you. It will help you use different techniques in the teaching of reading comprehension, writing, and composing using a great variety of resources of free and open source software available in the Web and interesting websites as well as social networks.

Conventions

In this book, you will find a number of styles of text that distinguish between different kinds of information. Here are some examples of these styles, and an explanation of their meaning.

New terms and **important words** are shown in bold. Words that you see on the screen, in menus or dialog boxes for example, appear in our text like this: "clicking the **Next** button moves you to the next screen".

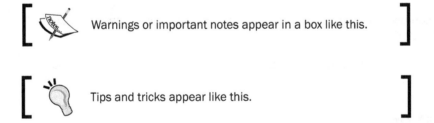

Warnings or important notes appear in a box like this.

Tips and tricks appear like this.

Reader feedback

Feedback from our readers is always welcome. Let us know what you think about this book—what you liked or may have disliked. Reader feedback is important for us to develop titles that you really get the most out of.

To send us general feedback, simply drop an email to feedback@packtpub.com, and mention the book title in the subject of your message.

If there is a book that you need and would like to see us publish, please send us a note in the **SUGGEST A TITLE** form on `www.packtpub.com` or email `suggest@packtpub.com`.

If there is a topic that you have expertise in and you are interested in either writing or contributing to a book, see our author guide on `www.packtpub.com/authors`.

Customer support

Now that you are the proud owner of a Packt book, we have a number of things to help you to get the most from your purchase.

Errata

Although we have taken every care to ensure the accuracy of our contents, mistakes do happen. If you find a mistake in one of our books—maybe a mistake in text or code—we would be grateful if you would report this to us. By doing so, you can save other readers from frustration, and help us to improve subsequent versions of this book. If you find any errata, please report them by visiting `http://www.packtpub.com/support`, selecting your book, clicking on the **let us know** link, and entering the details of your errata. Once your errata are verified, your submission will be accepted and the errata added to any list of existing errata. Any existing errata can be viewed by selecting your title from `http://www.packtpub.com/support`.

Piracy

Piracy of copyright material on the Internet is an ongoing problem across all media. At Packt, we take the protection of our copyright and licenses very seriously. If you come across any illegal copies of our works in any form on the Internet, please provide us with the location address or website name immediately so that we can pursue a remedy.

Please contact us at `copyright@packtpub.com` with a link to the suspected pirated material.

We appreciate your help in protecting our authors, and our ability to bring you valuable content.

Questions

You can contact us at `questions@packtpub.com` if you are having a problem with any aspect of the book, and we will do our best to address it.

1

Connecting Ideas

Connecting the ideas of our students is one of the most difficult tasks to carry out in the teaching process. This is primarily because they find it very hard to do. Therefore, these types of Exercises using Moodle 1.9.5 will help you to overcome such situations. Your students will be attracted to the proposed assignments because they are quite appealing.

In this chapter, we will cover the following topics:

- Matching sentences
- Unjumbling and connecting sentences
- Using Twitter and Facebook for surveys
- Brainstorming ideas using Forums
- Answering a quiz designed in a lesson
- Uploading pictures from Microsoft Word
- Connecting events—uploading drawings from Microsoft Word
- Linking to a website and writing a description

Introduction

In this chapter, you will be able to design several types of Exercises concerning reading comprehension, writing, and composing through Moodle 1.9.5. You will learn to use Facebook, Twitter, Wikis, and Forums so that students can interact among themselves while completing the Moodle courses. Apart from that, you will be given some hints on how to develop the same activity in another way using resources from the Web 2.0, and uploading clipart and drawings from Microsoft Word.

In this virtual classroom, students will enrich the use of connectors. For starters, they will work with connectors on simple activities—for example, they will connect sentences. Then they will use those connectors in different Exercises. These connectors were used previously in a simpler way. I designed the activities in such a way that the level of difficulty increases throughout the book along with the writing of the students. That is because I believe in the premise that students have to read in order to write. We have to bear in mind that on the one hand, reading is a passive and receptive skill, while on the other hand, writing is an active or productive one.

As a teacher, I always add a personal touch to any methodology, Exercise, or suggestion, and the recipes in this book are the results. I hope that you enjoy them. You can follow my instructions or add a personal touch to any recipe. Let's Moodle it!

Matching sentences

In this Exercise, we are going to match pairs of sentences. We should focus on connectors, as the difficult or misleading part of the suggested Exercise is that the sentences tend to be confusing. The students will change the meaning if they match them with the wrong connector. I propose to do this task using Moodle 1.9.5 and Hot Potatoes.

 Hot Potatoes is a freeware, whose suite includes six applications, enabling you to create interactive multiple-choice, short-answer, jumbled-sentence, crossword, matching or ordering and gap-fill Exercises for the World Wide Web. We will discuss it further at the end of the recipe.

Getting ready

Let's create an Exercise to work on compound sentences. The connectors are to vary according to the age of the students. Since this is the first recipe, we are going to create a course in Moodle called Reading Comprehension, Writing, and Composing. In this course, we are going to add the foregoing activities in the book. Afterwards, you have to turn editing on (remember that on the top right margin of the screen it has to say **Turn editing off**).

How to do it...

Enter the course that you have already created and choose the Weekly outline section that you want to add the activity to. Then follow these steps:

1. Click on the drop-down box in **Add an activity** and select **Quiz**.
2. In the **Name** block write the title of the quiz, and in **Introduction**, broaden what the target of the Exercise is, as shown in the following screenshot:

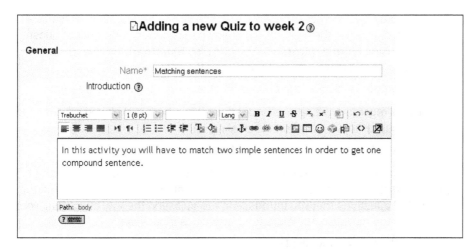

3. At the bottom of the **Introduction** block, a yellow icon appears with a question mark and a keyboard next to it. It is **HTML Editor Shortcut Keys**. If you click on it, a table appears, and if you scroll down the table, you can see all the shortcuts available along with their explanations (however, they don't work on all browsers or OS systems), as shown in the following screenshot:

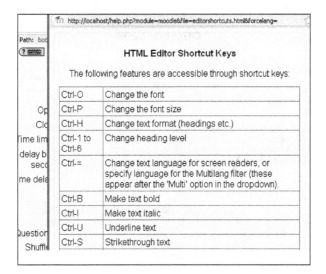

4. In the **Timing** block, there are some options such as enabling an opening and closing date for the quiz—if you want to do so, you will have to uncheck **Disable** and you are allowed to use these options. **Time limit** works if you **enable** the block.

5. In the **Display** box, you have three options: **Questions per page**, which can be **Unlimited** (this is not the best option) or you can choose the number of questions to be shown using **Shuffle questions**. You can also **Shuffle within questions**. This will vary according to the way you want to design the activity.

6. In the **Attempts** block, you can choose whether or not to limit the attempts.

7. **Grades:** As regards grading method, I think it is a personal choice according to the type of group or activity that you are dealing with.

8. **Common module settings** are really optional.

9. Scrolling down, **Overall feedback** appears that is to be completed according to your group of students. It contains the percentages that are quite individualized, the amount of questions that you introduce in the quiz, and the way of marking your Exercises. You may also add more feedback fields if necessary.

10. Finally click on **Save and display**.

How it works...

Now another screen appears in which you will have to click on the drop-down menu next to **Create new question**. Then choose **Matching** (which is the title of our activity), as shown in the following screenshot:

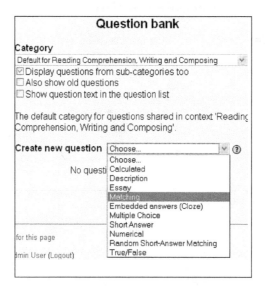

Now we can design our matching activity by following the next steps:

1. You have to complete the **Question name**.

2. As regards **Question text,** you can write something related to the activity or write the same as **Question name**.

3. In **General feedback,** you can give information about the usage of connectors that you are going to deal with in the activity.

4. Next, add the questions. There appear three available choices to fill in. You may add more (I always do). By the way, the question does not need to be a question per se, but half of the sentence, as we are doing a matching sentences activity.

5. Another possibility that Moodle provides is to complete one more answer to mislead our students. Instead of having an even matching activity, we have an extra one which is not used, as shown in the following screenshot:

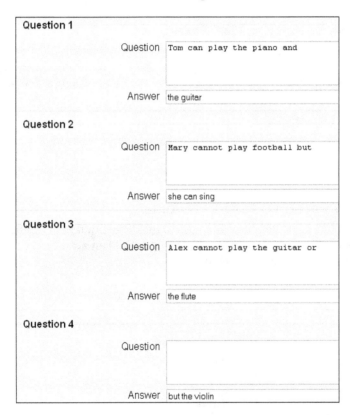

6. Now click on **Save changes**. After that, go back to the course and try the activity yourself.

Let's Moodle it! Your quiz has to appear on your Moodle course, as shown in the following screenshot:

There's more...

We can also carry out the same type of activity through Hot Potatoes and upload it to our Moodle course.

Carry out the activity in Hot Potatoes

We can also carry out this type of quiz in Hot Potatoes using JMatch (the green potato) and uploading it in Moodle 1.9.5. It is much simpler to design a matching activity in Hot Potatoes than in Moodle. Apart from that, JMatch activities are quite appealing to the eye.

Hot Potatoes website

Downloading the Hot Potatoes software is quite easy (if you already have Moodle you can download without any difficulty whatsoever). The website is `http://hotpot.uvic.ca/#downloads`.

Showing Hot Potatoes Quiz in Moodle

Once you have installed Hot Potatoes, you have to make sure that Moodle has been set up to display it as an activity. In other words, by clicking on **Add an activity**, the following option should appear, as shown in the next screenshot:

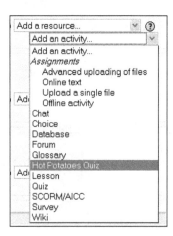

If you do not have the option **Hot Potatoes Quiz**, you have to ask for the admin rights or the required access in order to follow these steps:

1. Go to the first page where all the courses available are displayed. In **Site Administration,** click on **Modules**.

2. Next, click on **Activities** and then on **Manage activities**.

3. **Hot Potatoes Quiz** has a closed eye symbol and we are going to click on it to open. This means that it was hidden, and now it is displayed. The same happens with the other activities. These steps are shown in the following screenshot:

Site Administration	Activities					
Notifications						
Users	**Activity module**	**Activities**	**Version**	**Hide/Show**	**Delete**	**Settings**
Courses	Assignment	0	2007101511	👁	Delete	Settings
Grades	Chat	0	2009031100	👁	Delete	Settings
Location	? Choice	0	2007101509	👁	Delete	
Language	Database	0	2007101514	👁	Delete	Settings
Modules	Exercise	0	2007110500	👁	Delete	
Activities	Forum	1	2007101513			Settings
Manage activities	Glossary	0	2007101509	👁	Delete	Settings
Assignment	Hot Potatoes Quiz	1	2007101513	👁‍🗨	Delete	Settings
Chat	Journal	0	2007101509	👁	Delete	
Database	Label	0	2007101510	👁	Delete	
Forum	LAMS	0	2007101509	👁	Delete	Settings
Glossary	Lesson	0	2008112601	👁	Delete	
LAMS	Quiz	1	2007101511	👁	Delete	Settings
Quiz	Resource	0	2007101509	👁	Delete	Settings
Resource	SCORM/AICC	0	2007110502	👁	Delete	Settings
SCORM/AICC	Survey	0	2007101509	👁	Delete	
Blocks	Wiki	0	2007101509	👁	Delete	
Filters	Workshop	0	2007101509	👁	Delete	
Security						
Appearance						
Front Page						
Server						
Networking						
Reports						
Miscellaneous						

Search

Admin bookmarks

Creating a matching activity in Hot Potatoes

Let's create a quiz in Hot Potatoes using JMatch and upload it in our Moodle course. After downloading Hot Potatoes and displaying it, let's take advantage of its resources! I have designed the following activity for our students to connect their ideas. After clicking on JMatch, you have to fill in the blanks, as shown in the following screenshot:

Title	Connecting Ideas	
	Left (ordered) items	**Right (jumbled) items**
1	He can play football and	many other sports.
2	He cannot study at night because	he is very tired.
3	He would study if	he had time.
4	He will give you a lift as soon as	he finishes.
5	What about his coming to	our party tonight?

1. After filling in the blanks, we are going to save the file in order to upload it into our Moodle course. Click on **File** and select **Save as**, then give a name to your file. Remember to write a name without spaces so that it is easier to work with later.

2. After that, you are going to save it as a web page. Click on **File** and select **Create a web page.** Then choose **Drag/Drop format** and click on **Save**. You may try this activity and click on **View the Exercise in my browser,** or just click on **Nothing** and save the file.

3. Let's upload the activity into Moodle and go back to our Moodle course.

4. Choose the Weekly outline section where you want to display the activity.

5. Choose **Add an activity | Hot Potatoes Quiz**.

6. Complete the **Name** block, click on the drop-down box and choose **Specific text,** else it will just get the name from the Hot Potatoes Quiz.

7. After that, click on **Choose or upload a file** .Then you will have to click on **Upload a file**.

8. Click on **Browse** and choose your file. After that, click on **Upload a file** again and then click on **Choose**.

9. Click on **Save and display**. Now you can do the quiz!

Unjumbling and connecting sentences

With this recipe, you are going to design a reading comprehension activity carried out in Moodle 1.9.5. We are going to link to the webpage of `http://www.biography.com` to check the biography of Lewis Carroll. Students are to read his biography, and then they are going to order the sentences into a paragraph. You can choose another webpage or a story instead of a biography. I found this quite appealing—a very important characteristic to bear in mind when choosing a webpage. Let's Moodle it!

Getting ready

As mentioned previously, I have just chosen the webpage in which we can read the biography of Lewis Carroll. Later, we have to unjumble his biography. The best way to do it is through Hot Potatoes. We are going to link to a webpage so that students can have hints, though they can do it in Hot Potatoes by clicking on the word **Hint** when they are stuck in an activity.

First, you are to go through the Lewis Carroll biography yourself and rewrite and mix it so that you can create the Exercise in Hot Potatoes. This time you are going to use JMix—the light blue potato. You are going to complete the main text in the correct order, and later you are going to alternate the sentences, as shown in the following screenshot:

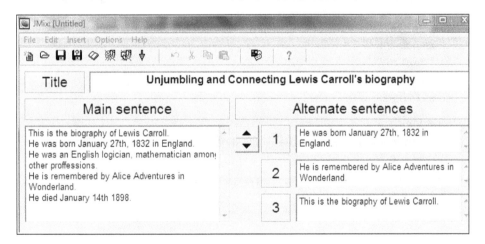

How to do it...

We have just created the activity in Hot Potatoes. However, as a contrast to the activity created in the first recipe, I am going to add a link to a website through the activity. So let's do it!

1. Type the words **Lewis Carroll's biography,** as we are linking to the website of his biography. Choose **Insert | Link | Link to Web URL**. The following screenshot appears:

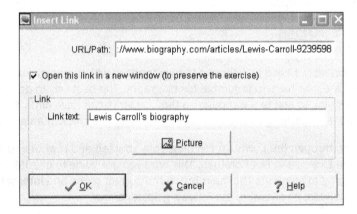

2. The **Link text** block will be completed automatically because those words were chosen to link to the website. What you have to complete is the **URL/Path** connecting to the website.

3. You may choose whether to **Open this link in a new window** or not. I always do this so as to preserve the activity in another window.

4. Click on **OK**.

5. In the **Title** box, some words that you did not type will appear. This is the link to the website.

6. Save the file. Click on **File**, select **Save as**, complete the filename block, and then click on **Save**.

How it works...

After creating the activity in Hot Potatoes and linking it to a website, we can upload it in Moodle as previously done in the first recipe. This can be done by using the following steps:

1. Let's upload the activity into Moodle. Select **Add an activity | Hot Potatoes | Quiz**.

2. Click on **Choose or upload a file.** Click on **Upload a file | Browse** and then select your file. Afterwards, click on **Upload a file** again and then click on **Choose**. Now click on **Save and display**.

3. You can do the quiz! The quiz title will appear with the words **Lewis Carroll's biography** in blue and it will be underlined as shown in the following screenshot:

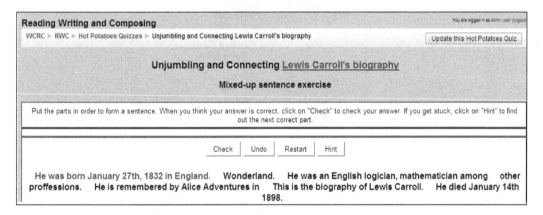

Using Twitter and Facebook for a survey

In this recipe, we are going to create a survey Exercise in Moodle. In this Exercise, students can update the content of a table about their likes and dislikes regarding books they have already read. We are going to create two links to websites where they can ask more people about this so that they can gather more data for the survey. Apart from that, they can write a report on this topic later. Let's Moodle it!

Getting ready

We are going to create an activity in which all the students can give their opinion and update the same table as soon as they know about people's likes and dislikes on books. This can be done using Wiki. Let's Moodle it!

How to do it...

We are going to enter the course and select the Weekly outline section where we want to add this activity for designing.

1. Click on **Add an activity** and select the **Wiki** option, as shown in the following screenshot:

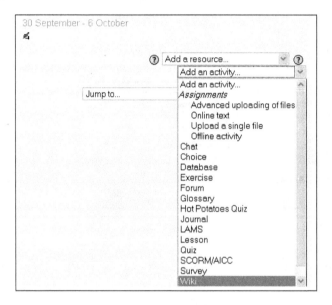

2. Complete the **Name** block with the title of the survey that the students are going to execute.

3. In the **Summary** block, broaden the target of the activity. You can add the links to the websites. Your students can use these links to complete the survey.

4. Create two links to websites: one to Facebook.com and the other to Twitter.com.

5. When you type the title in the **Summary** block, highlight the word Twitter and create a link to its website by clicking on the chain icon of the editor, as shown in the following screenshot:

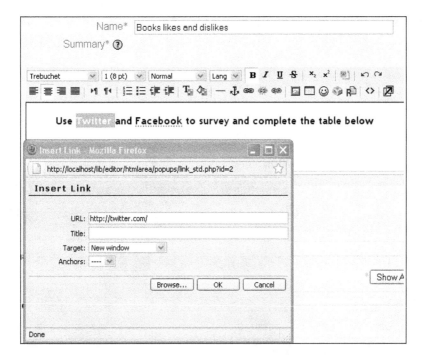

6. In **URL,** write the name of the website and in **Target** choose **New window**, as shown in the previous screenshot so that students can go on working with both windows. Then click on **OK**.

7. The same steps are to be followed when linking to Facebook, but you have to highlight the word Facebook and write its website address, which is http://www.facebook.com/.

8. Click on **Save and display**.

How it works...

After saving the changes in Wiki, we have to prepare the activity that our students must complete. You have several options, such as choosing the books to ask about, requesting people to give the names of those books, or just changing the topic of the survey. In this case, you will be giving a personal touch to the activity that I propose. Follow these steps to finish designing the activity:

1. The following screen will appear and you are going to design the table that your students are going to complete.

2. To insert the table, you have to click on its icon that lies between the mountain and the smiling face.

3. You are going to need a table consisting of **2 Rows** and **3 Cols**. Once you enter the values for number of rows and columns, click on **OK**. Your activity will be displayed, as shown in the following screenshot:

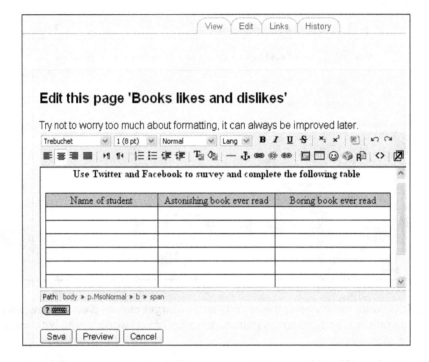

4. At the bottom of the table, write another title: Write a paragraph that states the results of the survey.

5. After writing the activity, click on **Save**.

6. Then go back to the course.

7. The activity should appear on the Weekly outline section.

Make sure that that whenever the students have to complete the task, they have to click on **Edit** so that they can complete the activity, as shown in the next screenshot:

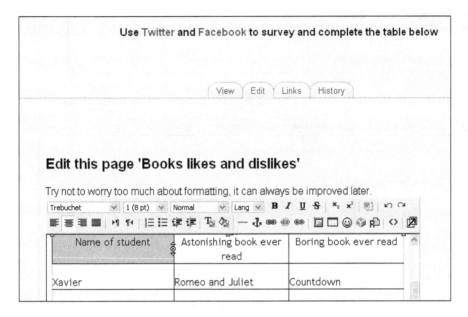

There's more...

There is an organization which protects the rights and privacy of students. Before designing this type of activity, it would be advisable to take this into consideration.

Protecting Students' Rights and Privacy

The **Family Educational Rights and Privacy Act** (**FERPA**) protects students' rights and privacy. Disclosing personal information of the student should be consented by the parents as well as from the school. You can read more in the following website `http://www2.ed.gov/policy/gen/guid/fpco/ferpa/index.html`.

Brainstorming ideas using Forums

In this recipe, we are going to connect different images. We are going to use Forums so that all the students can comment on two different things, and we are going to guide their writing with general questions. I propose that the title gives them a hint on what they are going to deal with, but the images that they are going to see are two websites with information. You may wonder, 'Why?' Remember the premise of reading before writing. They are to read about two different places and then they are going to write about them. A way to enhance the students' vocabulary is to make them read and give them hints on it.

Getting ready

We are going to design a Forum activity. We enter the course and select the Weekly outline section in which we want to add the activity. Let's Moodle it!

How to do it...

To design the activity previously introduced, you are going to follow these steps:

1. Click on **Add an activity** and select **Forum**, as shown in the following screenshot:

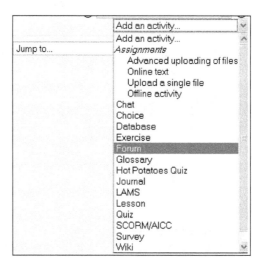

2. In the **Forum name** block, write the title of the activity, and in **Forum introduction**, write what they are going to do. Visit the two websites, and after visitation, answer the guiding questions (it is somewhat similar to the 'Six Thinking Hats Technique' by Edward de Bono).

3. We are going to create a link to the two websites. One of them is `http://www.statueofliberty.org/`, which is a link to the official website of the Statue of Liberty, and the other is a link to `http://www.yosemite.org/`, which is a link to the official website of Yosemite National Park.

4. Highlight the words **Website number one**, click on the **Insert Web Link** icon, and then complete the block. In **Target**, select **New window**.

5. Repeat the same process for **Website number two**, and create a link to the Yosemite National Park website.

6. This activity is displayed in the next screenshot:

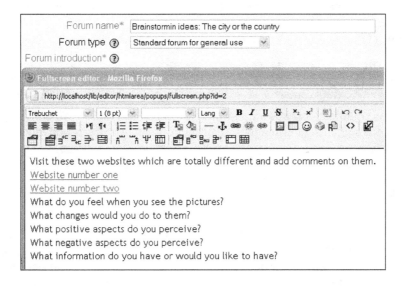

7. Click on **Save and return to course**.

How it works...

When students click on the activity, it appears as shown in the next screenshot:

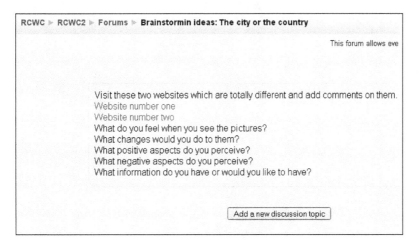

Students are to click on **Add a new discussion topic,** and an editor appears where they can write the answers to the questions given there. They can also keep those websites open in different windows so that they don't have to close the activity.

The aim is that each student should comment on these two different places explaining what they think. They are expected to write simple paragraphs, as they will write articles or descriptions in further chapters. In order to answer these questions, they will have to think and use some of the vocabulary that they have already seen in the websites.

Answering a quiz designed in a Lesson

Answering a quiz may lead towards a well-written personal description. We are going to design a quiz so that our students can write their biography or just their habits and routines, including their personal likes and dislikes. They can answer questions about themselves or we can add a link to a website showing the life of a famous person so that they write about him or her.

Getting ready

We are going to design a guided writing activity using a Lesson. First of all, we are going to design the activity so that our students write about themselves. Then we will put in details about a famous person, and finally add a link about that person's life to the website. We enter the course and select the Weekly outline section in which we want to add the activity. Let's Moodle it!

How to do it...

You are going to design this activity in a Lesson, so you have to click on **Add an activity** and select **Lesson**, as shown in the next screenshot:

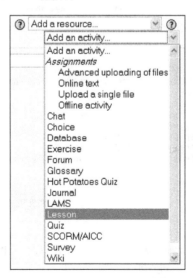

1. Complete the **Name** block by writing the title of the activity, as shown in the next screenshot:

2. You can either change the other items or keep them unchanged according to your choice.
3. Click on **Save and display**.

How it works...

Then what do you do? You have to write questions for guided writing! A screen appears with four options. You have to select **Add a Question Page** and write the questions for guided writing. These are the steps to follow:

1. Click on **Add a Question Page**.
2. Choose **Essay**.
3. Write a title in the **Page title** block.
4. Complete the **Page contents** with the questions for the guided writing, as shown in the next screenshot:

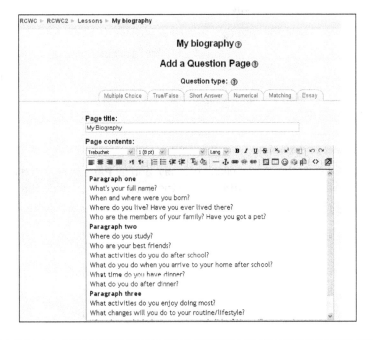

5. Click on **Add a question page**.

6. Then go back to the course.

7. Your students can write their biography!

There's more...

You may also design another similar type of activity, but in this case students can write about the biography of a famous person.

Writing somebody's biography using a link to a website

You are going to add a link to a website so that students can write a biography about a famous person. You can ask students to rewrite the biography of Amelia Earhart in a simpler way. They are going to answer questions similar to the ones designed for their biography, or you may change them.

You are going to follow these steps:

1. Click on **Add an activity** and choose **Lesson**.

2. Complete the **Name** block by writing **Amelia Earhart's biography** in this block.

3. Scroll down the page and complete the block **Pop-up to file or web page** by entering the name of the website `http://www.ameliaearhart.com/about/bio.html`, as shown in the following screenshot:

4. Click on **Save and display**.

5. Select **Add a Question Page**, click on **Essay**, and fill **Page title** with the title of the activity. Then fill out **Page contents** with the questions that guide the writing.

6. Click on **Add a Questions Page**.

7. Go back to the course.

When students want to do an activity, the difference between this activity and the previous one is that they are going to see the **Linked media** icon. When they click on **Click here to view,** the website link will appear, as shown in the following screenshot:

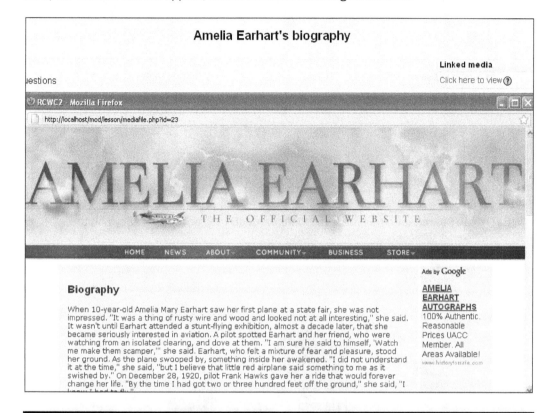

Empty book, great story: upload pictures from Microsoft Word

Isolated pictures of different items are to be presented on an empty book. The idea is that this empty book, which is full of different objects, should have a story written. The items are of any kind. Students are to write a story using these images and connectors.

Getting ready

We are going to design a guided writing activity through a Journal. We are going to design the activity so that our students write a story out of some pictures. We enter the course and choose the Weekly outline section in which we want to add the activity. Let's Moodle it!

How to do it...

Before creating the activity in Moodle, we have to create the file with the images to upload. In this case, we are going to do it in Microsoft Word. These are the steps to follow in case you have created similar files. After you have opened the software, create a new document and follow these steps:

1. Click on **Insert** and choose **Clip Art**, as shown in the following screenshot:

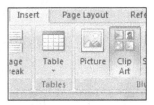

2. In the **Search for** block, write the word **book** and click on **Go**, as shown in the following screenshot:

3. Find an image—in this case, the empty book—and add other clipart images on it to guide the story that the students are going to write.

4. Look for the pictures to insert inside the book so that students can write the story. Select a rose, a couple, and a car.

5. Repeat the same process and create a picture document.

6. Select the pictures from Microsoft Word, copy and paste them in Paint, Inkscape, or Image Editor, and copy them in .png, .jpeg, or .jpg formats. This is shown in the following screenshot:

How it works...

Choose the Weekly outline section where you want to carry out the activity. You are going to design this activity in a Journal. It is a good option to carry out this activity. Choose **Add an activity** and click on **Journal**, as shown in the following screenshot:

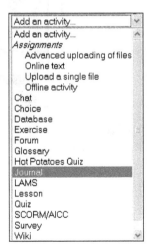

1. Fill the **Journal name** block with the title of the activity.

2. In the **Journal question**, write the description of the activity and add the pictures on the empty book (by empty book, I mean a book with pictures without any text whatsoever). Copy and paste the file we created using Word in Paint. To upload the pictures, click on the icon to insert a picture.

3. Click on **Browse** to find the file.

4. When you have found the file, click on **Open**.

5. Click on **Upload**. Click on the image's link and its URL is automatically inserted into the **Image URL** block.

6. Complete the **Alternate text** block as shown in the following screenshot:

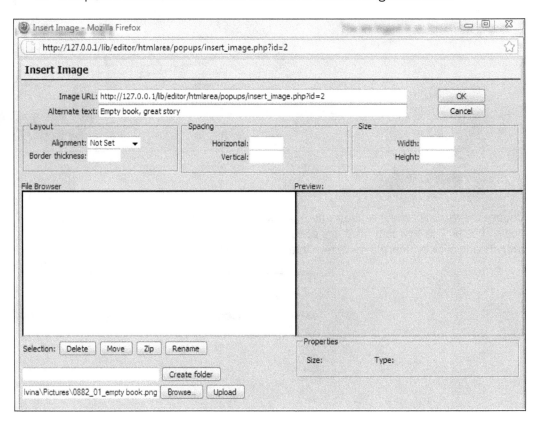

7. Click on the file's name that you have just uploaded and then click on **OK**. That's it! The empty book is in Moodle, as shown in the following screenshot:

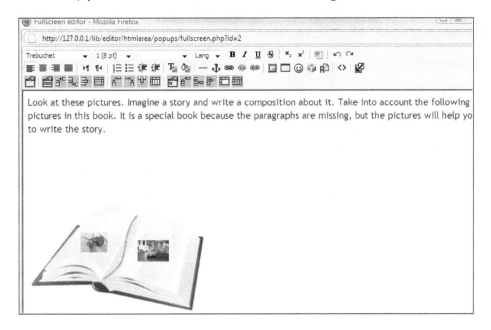

8. We can change the size of the picture as we do in Microsoft Word by clicking on it and resizing it.

9. Once you are happy with the image, click on **Save and return to course**.

10. The activity is ready for your students to write!

Connecting stairs: Uploading drawings from Microsoft Word

In this recipe, I have adapted what is known as "staircase writing". It is what occurs to you as you descend stairs at the end of the evening. The French call it "L'espirit d'escalier". We are not going to tell the students to go down the stairs with their notebook to write a beautiful story. Instead, my proposal is to draw stairs with keywords and events. We are going to draw a set of stairs in Microsoft Word, and then upload it to Moodle. Let's Moodle it!

Getting ready

We are going to open a new file in Microsoft Word. While doing so, we are going to draw a staircase, and then add some key, linking words. The main purpose is to supply our students with enough tools to gather the data and write a beautiful piece of writing.

How to do it...

First of all, you are going to open a new file and draw the staircase. Then add the key, linking words that you want your students to use. To draw the staircase, you can decide either to draw it or to upload a clipart in Word. In this case, I decided to draw it and here are the steps to follow:

1. Choose **Insert Shapes** and click on the **Elbow Connector**.

2. Draw the staircase using the elbow connector. After drawing it, you can add 3D effects so that it looks like a staircase. Then add a title and the description of the activity, as shown in the following screenshot:

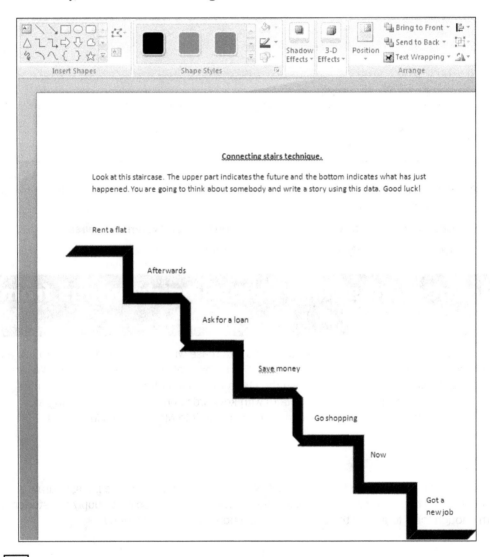

3. This is what you have to show your students so that they can write, bearing in mind the order of the events.

How it works...

The activity is already done, but in Microsoft Word. What we need to do is upload this activity in Moodle and let our students write. These are the steps that you need to follow in order to design this activity. We are going to use two types of activities; static and dynamic. The static activity is to upload the Microsoft Word file into Moodle and the dynamic activity is to create a Journal and a link towards the Microsoft Word file so that students are to read the file and write the activity in Moodle through the Journal. It is not as difficult as it sounds. Let's Moodle it!

1. Click on **Add a resource** and select **Link to a file or a website**.
2. In the **Name** block, write **Connecting stairs**.
3. In the summary, you can write the description of the activity.
4. Click on **Choose or upload a file**.
5. Then click on **Upload a file**.
6. Click on **Browse** and look for your file.
7. Select your file, click on it, and then click on **Open**.
8. Click on **Upload a file** again.
9. Your file has just uploaded. Now click on **Choose** as shown in the following screenshot:

10. Click on **Save and return to course**.
11. You have done part of this task. What you now need to do is create the dynamic activity for the students so that they can use this file.

There's more...

We can also create a link to the file designed in Microsoft Word. We can do this using the insert a link icon.

Creating a link with a Microsoft file

We have to link the file in Microsoft Word that we have just uploaded into Moodle with an activity. By default, this activity doesn't allow us to upload a file. But we are going to do it using a link. Follow these steps:

1. Click on **Add an activity**, and select **Journal**.
2. Complete the **Journal name** block with the title of the activity.
3. Write the description of the activity in the **Journal question** block. Highlight the words **Connecting stairs technique** in the **Journal question** block and click on the chain icon.
4. Click on **Browse** and click on the file you want to upload.
5. Write a title in the **Title** block.
6. In the **Target** block, choose **New window**, as shown in the next screenshot:

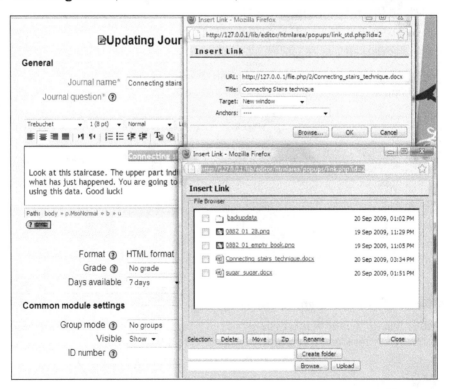

7. Click on **OK**.

8. Click on **Save and return to course**.

9. The activity is ready to work with.

Linking to websites and writing about an endangered animal

In this recipe, I suggest that you write about an endangered animal. For example, the first animal that comes to my mind whenever people mention the topic, "endangered species," is the Panda bear. Therefore, I am going to design this very simple and short activity about Panda bears. What I propose is a link to the same website—first watching a video and then reading an article.

Getting ready

We have already used the Journal, so this is a very simple activity. What we are going to do is select which endangered animal we are going to deal with. In this case, as I have already mentioned, it is the Panda bear. The chosen website is the `http://www.national geographic.com`, which gives us accurate data about this topic. Therefore, we are going to choose in which Weekly outline section we want to design the activity. Let's Moodle it!

How to do it...

After choosing the Weekly outline section in which you want to display the activity, you are going to follow these steps:

1. Click on **Add an activity** and choose **Journal**.

2. Complete the **Journal name** block.

3. Then complete the **Journal question** block with the description of the activity.

4. Write the words **Pandas' video** and **Pandas' article.** You are going to use the same procedure for both links to the website.

5. Highlight the words **Pandas' video** and click on the chain icon, then complete the link to the website window, as shown in the following screenshot:

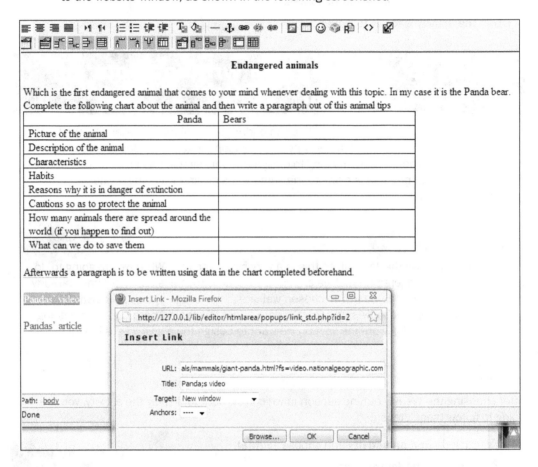

6. Remember to choose **New window** in **Target** and then click on **OK**.

7. Follow the same procedure for **Pandas' article.**

8. Click on **Save and return to course**.

9. The activity is ready for your students to work.

How it works...

When your students click on the activity, they can see the words underlined **Pandas' video** and **Pandas' article**. After clicking on those words, they will read the article and watch the video about Panda bears. In this way, they can gather data and write the article about Pandas taking into account the keywords. They can also express their opinion about taking care of the Panda bear.

2
Matching Pictures and Text

Matching pictures and text are part of the reading comprehension skill that our students develop by reading different types of texts—for instance, articles, poems, song lyrics, dialogues, and comic strips, among others. Whenever the reader is trying to picture the effect of the text in his or her mind's eye, it might be quite different from what another reader might imagine. This is understandable because a reader's imagination may change according to several factors such as interpretation of the text, their point of view, and so on. The reason we ask students to incorporate pictures, paragraphs, and flowcharts using Web 2.0 while working with comprehension is to brighten their ideas with regard to writing and composing. Finally, after matching images and text, we can work the other way round by inserting images into beautifully written pieces of text.

In this chapter, we will cover the following activities:

- ▶ Picturing comprehension
- ▶ Matching text to speech bubbles of strip comics
- ▶ Picture paragraph matching
- ▶ Sceneries and possible stories through flowcharts
- ▶ Working with painting—Salvador Dali's art
- ▶ Choosing a book by its cover
- ▶ Advising posters
- ▶ Cooking recipes

Introduction

In this chapter, you will be able to design several types of Exercises for reading comprehension, writing, and composing using Moodle 1.9.5 and Web 2.0. Reading comprehension will not be tested in a traditional way, but through imaginative and appealing activities. Pictures enhance and appeal to the students to work and brighten up their homework. Besides, we ought to take advantage of our virtual classroom and its increasing resources.

In this virtual classroom, we are going to let the imagination of our students fly so that they can imagine what they never thought they could. First, they will match pictures to texts and put them in order; later the Exercises that I propose are the opposite based on the pictures, they have to write.

The writing of the students is enriched because they read before writing. As a result, their vocabulary increases. That is the reason why reading is quite important. Though reading is a passive skill, through this skill, students incorporate a lot of vocabulary and idiomatic expressions. Consequently, we turn a passive skill into an active one. By matching texts and pictures, they associate the new vocabulary with the image and they can learn it more quickly.

As I stated in the previous chapter, I always add a personal touch to any methodology, Exercise, or suggestion. So, you may find these activities as tips for your future Assignments. Let's Moodle it!

Picturing comprehension

In this task, we are going to match pictures and poems. What I find really interesting is that students read different types of texts as stated before. We are to focus on comprehension, and understanding how other people picture what they read. The students will not understand the poems if they match them with the wrong picture. I propose to carry out this activity in Moodle 1.9.5 using the Choice activity and Forum so that students can interact among themselves and state the reason they have made that choice.

Getting ready

Let's choose three poems that are related to one topic. The students will have to read them thoroughly and match them to three pictures that we are going to create according to the way we picture the poem. The poems are to vary according to the age of the students. In this case, we are going to work with three poems from the British Council website: http//britishcouncil.com. Students can read and listen to the poems, as the said website allows these options. There is also a link to a dictionary, so if there happens to be a word that they do not understand, they can look up the meaning. Let's Moodle it!

How to do it...

Enter the course and choose the Weekly outline section in which you want to add an activity. Then follow these steps:

1. Click on the drop-down box in **Add an activity** and select **Choice**.

2. In the **Choice name** block, write the title of the activity, and in **Choice text**, explain to the students what they have to do.

3. Write the name of the three poems and label them as **Poem A**, **Poem B**, and **Poem C**. After the poems are labeled, create a link to their websites by clicking on the chain icon as shown in the following screenshot:

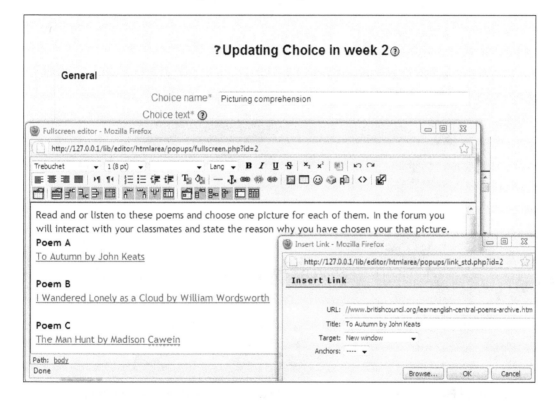

4. Complete the **Insert Link** boxes, one for each poem as shown in the previous screenshot. Make sure that you select the **New window** in the **Target** block.

5. Click on **OK**.

6. Repeat the same process for each poem.

7. We will upload the three images afterwards.

The name of the chosen poem is shown in the screenshot.

How it works...

After linking to the three websites to make the reading and listening comprehension activity of our students more entertaining, we are going to upload three images for these poems. An alternate option is to work with two or four pictures so that they can select uneven pairs. As you have already noticed, the poems mention nature in different ways. Therefore, we are going to choose nature elements in our pictures. We are going to upload pictures from `http://commons.wikimedia.org`. Follow these steps:

1. Enter the website that I have already mentioned:
    `http://commons.wikimedia.org`.

2. In the **Search** block, enter the name of the picture that you are looking for, as shown in the following screenshot:

3. Write **Picture one** in the **Choice** block and click on the **Insert picture** icon.

4. Right-click on the image you want to insert and copy the image location.

5. Go back to the Moodle course, and paste the image location in the **Image URL** block.

6. Complete the **Alternative text** block and click on **OK**. The image is in our Moodle course. Repeat the same process twice.

7. Complete the **Choice** blocks with alternative choices for matching the poems and the pictures—for example, **Poem A Picture 1**, **Poem B Picture 2**, and **Poem C Picture 3**, as shown in the next screenshot:

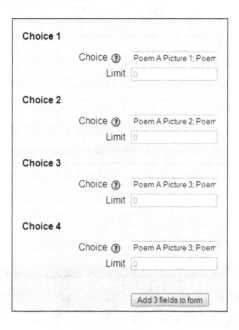

8. Several options appear, which are optional for your activity. You may activate them or not.

9. You can add three more fields to the form if necessary. Afterwards, click on **Save and display**.

There's more...

In the same Weekly outline section that we have introduced the previous activity, we are going to include the Forum activity with the following title, **Justifying the choices**.

Students justifying their choice in a Forum

Students will interact among themselves to give the reasons for their choices. This is also a way to check that they have understood what they have read. Apart from that, it is a writing activity that is productive, in contrast with all the passive ones which they have already done. Follow these steps:

1. Click on **Add an activity** and select **Forum**.

2. Complete the **Forum name** with the title previously suggested.

3. Complete the **Forum introduction** as shown in the following screenshot:

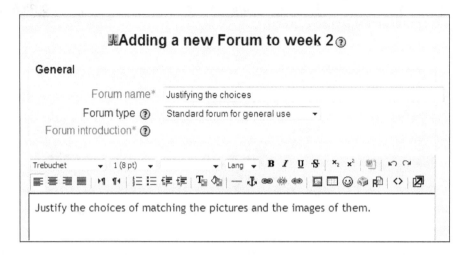

4. Click on **Save and return to course**.

Matching text to speech bubbles of comic strips

In this recipe, we will design a very simple comic strip in Microsoft Word using pictures from the website `http://www.sxc.hu` and speech bubbles from Microsoft Word. Later, we will copy and paste this comic strip in Paint (this comic strip is going to be out of sequence) and save it as a `.png` document, that is to say a picture file. Afterwards, we are going to carry out our matching activity in Moodle 1.9.5 with the comic strip on top of the activity. We can also ask our students to write a story based on the comic strip (they will have to place it in order) using the information in the speech bubbles. Let's Moodle it!

Getting ready

First of all, we are going to surf the website `http://www.sxc.hu` to get enough images to create a comic strip. When we enter the website, we will search for silhouette images, as these make it easier to let the imagination of our students fly away. So we are going to type **silhouette** in the search box and click on **Browse** as shown in the following screenshot:

Afterwards, we will choose six images containing the same or similar characters so that we can create a coherent comic strip. It will take some time, but the results will be quite rewarding. After selecting the pictures, right-click on the pictures and select **Copy.** Now paste the image in Microsoft Word. Repeat the same steps six times, as we are working with six images in this case.

How to do it...

We have just chosen the images to work with. The next step is to create the comic strip in Microsoft Word. You may be wondering how this can be done. It is quite simple. We are going to insert a table with only six columns. After the table is inserted, we are going to cut and paste the six images into the six columns of the table—that is, a separate column for each image. We have just created a comic strip as shown in the following screenshot:

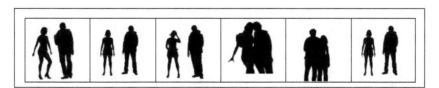

When concluding this comic strip, we will add speech bubbles that Microsoft Word provides. In the **Insert** menu, select the **Shapes** option as shown in the following screenshot:

We will choose some speech bubbles and cloud bubbles to create suspense and to allow our students to think freely. We can also add a **Flowchart banner** to include some text instead of speech from the characters of the comic strip. The result is displayed in the following screenshot:

How it works...

After creating the comic strip in Microsoft Word, we are going to design the activity in Moodle. In this case, we are going to work with a matching activity. So these are the steps to follow:

1. Click on **Add an activity** and select **Quiz**.

2. Complete the **Name** block with the name of the activity. In this case, you are going to write **Matching**.

3. In the **Introduction** block, you are going to write an introduction to the comic strip—for example, this is a comic strip about two people, a man called Nick and a woman called Nicole. The pictures are not in the correct order. You will have to arrange them in order when you perform the writing task.

4. Click on **Insert an image** icon and browse for the COMIC_STRIP.png file.

5. Then click on **Upload**.

6. Right-click on the image and select **Open file location**.

7. Copy the path and paste it in the **Image URL** block.

8. Complete the **Alternate text** block in case the image cannot be displayed.

9. Click on **OK**.

10. Complete the other blocks, and then click on **Save and display**.

    In the block, **Create a new question**, click on the drop-down box and select **Matching**.

11. You are going to complete the **Question name** block with the title of the activity. In this case, you can write Matching text to speech bubbles.

12. In the block, **Image to display**, click on the drop-down box and select the image that you want to upload. In this case, the image to be uploaded is the comic strip as shown in the following screenshot:

13. Complete the **Question** blocks as shown in the following screenshot:

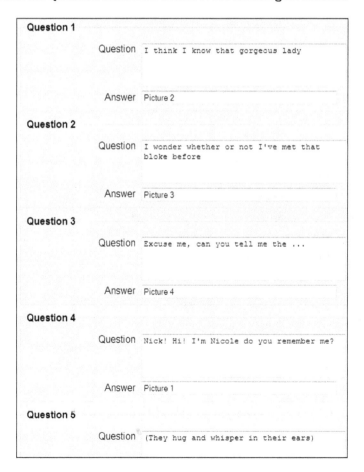

14. Click on **Save changes**.

15. Go back to the course.

16. If you want to try out the activity yourself, it should appear as follows:

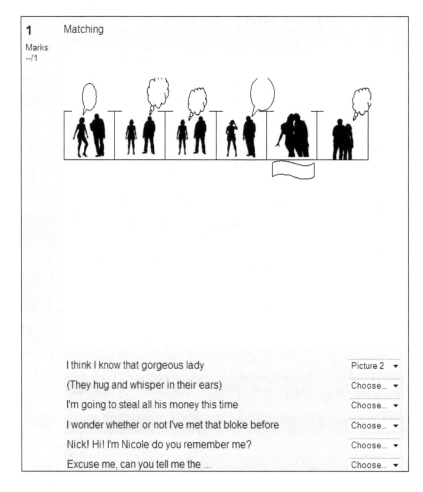

I think I know that gorgeous lady	Picture 2 ▾
(They hug and whisper in their ears)	Choose... ▾
I'm going to steal all his money this time	Choose... ▾
I wonder whether or not I've met that bloke before	Choose... ▾
Nick! Hi! I'm Nicole do you remember me?	Choose... ▾
Excuse me, can you tell me the ...	Choose... ▾

There's more...

We can insert a writing activity here. We can ask our students to write a story based on this comic strip.

Ordering and writing a story based on the comic strip

We can ask our students to write a story using the comic strip so that they can take full advantage of their own creations. Therefore, in my opinion, a Journal activity is appropriate. Besides, it is very simple and fast to design. In the same Weekly outline section or in the next one, we are going to add a Journal. Follow these steps:

1. Click on the drop-down box of **Add an activity** and select **Journal**.

2. Complete the **Journal name**. You can write 'Order the comic strip and write a story'.

3. Complete the **Journal question**. You can upload the same comic strip or a modified version with the speech bubbles written. (Follow the previous steps to do this).

4. Click on **Save and display**.

5. Go back to the course.

Picture paragraph matching

In this recipe, we are going to write six paragraphs in a Microsoft Word document. The students will have to match each paragraph with its corresponding picture that will be chosen from its clipart. We are going to carry out this activity in an Exercise in Moodle 1.9.5 so that students match the description to the pictures (an alternate option would be a Workshop). We are going to insert eight pictures, but we are not going to describe all of them. Our students have to complete this task by following the format of the previous descriptions. Let's Moodle it!

Getting ready

We are going to create an activity in Exercise so that we can upload the Microsoft Word document and design the activity there. The activity that we are going to create and upload into Moodle 1.9.5 is shown in the next screenshots:

Paragraph 1

This is the best place I've never thought it could possible exist outside my mind, but it does. The scenery is astonishing. Awesome! I whispered for myself. I was breathless. The sunset inspires quietness and relaxation.

Paragraph 2

What a portrait! A picture to remember what happened that day or what did not. The sea involves several feelings. I think that the little child is enjoying herself and she is spending such a beautiful time with her beloved family.

Paragraph 3

Funny, entertaining and noisy. Relaxation is out of the question in this picture. You do not need to listen because whenever you see this picture the sound can be heard in the silence. Teenagers are enjoying themselves too much. This is the way many of them spend their free time out of computers, using bigger ones, which simulate different types of vehicles and becoming famous characters.

Paragraph 4

Rain rain go away! You are about to spoil the outing! The scenery is gorgeous as well as astonishing. The lights reflect on the water, therefore there seems to be a city beneath the water, because of mirror effect of lights. The bridge above the incredible building is an extraordinary architecture.

Paragraph 5

Mother nature has just painted this picture. How crazy nature can be, there are many trees and they are all of different colors! The scenery is picturesque and unique. Relaxing and calming. Stress is out of the question. This is the place to wander and wonder what way to follow.

Paragraph 6

This is not a place to play but to gaze. The scenery is incredible. The trees are painted with the same color. Why can this happen? The water and the mountains are the perfect combination so as to enhance the picture. The sportsmen are peacefully listening to the sound of water.

How to do it...

We are going to enter the course and select the Weekly outline section where we want to add this activity so that we can design it:

1. Click on **Add an activity** and select the **Exercise** option.

2. Complete the **Title** block with the title of the activity.

3. In the **Maximum Size** block, select **16MB** because you are going to upload images as shown in the following screenshot:

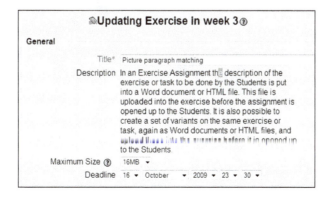

4. There are several options that you may change according to the activity that you want to design.

5. Click on **Save and display**.

6. Click on **Continue**.

7. Complete the following **Editing Assessment Elements** block (as shown in the following screenshot) or the way you want to assess your students:

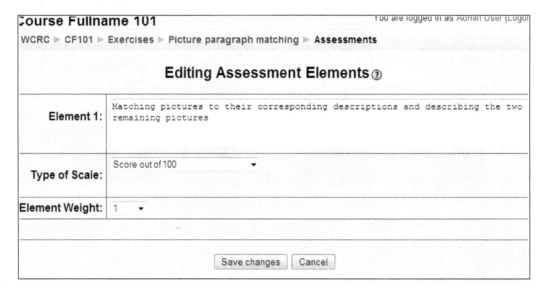

8. Click on **Save changes**.

9. Click on **Continue**.

How it works...

After saving the changes in the Exercise, we have to upload the activity that our students have to complete. The following screen appears where we have to upload the Exercise in Moodle 1.9.5. Go to **Set Up Exercise**, that is to say **Submit Exercise Description**, which will upload the Microsoft Word document into Moodle. Follow these steps to design the activity:

1. Click on **Set Up Exercise** and then on **Submit Exercise Description**, as shown in the following screenshot:

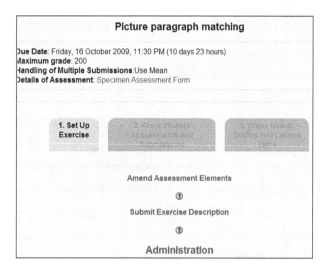

2. Click on **Browse** and select the file that you want to upload.
3. Write the title of the document in the **Title** block.
4. Click on **Upload this file**.
5. Click on **Continue** if your file is uploaded successfully.
6. Your activity is ready to work with.

Sceneries and possible stories through flowcharts

In this recipe, we are going to use Forums so that students can interact among themselves to check the matching of the flowcharts and stories. Afterwards, they will write the end of each story according to the pictures that they are shown. In this case, we are going to teach them how to write using keywords and flowcharts as guides. Though the Exercises here are not so long, we can design longer ones or more complex ones. We are going to use OpenOffice in this case, and then we will upload the images. The uploaded images will guide the students and help them in finishing their writing.

Getting ready

We are going to design the flowchart and the matching activity in OpenOffice (you can download it from the following website: `http://www.openoffice.org/`) so that we can upload it in Moodle 1.9.5. After uploading it, we will enter the course and select the Weekly outline section in which we want to add the activity. Let's Moodle it!

We are going to open OpenOffice and select the type of file as a text document (`.odt`). We will write a title and then click on the geometrical figures at the bottom of the page in order to create the flowchart. (Save the file in `.doc` format so that students who do not have OpenOffice may open the file in Microsoft Word or any other text editor). After this, we will complete the flowchart as shown in the following screenshot:

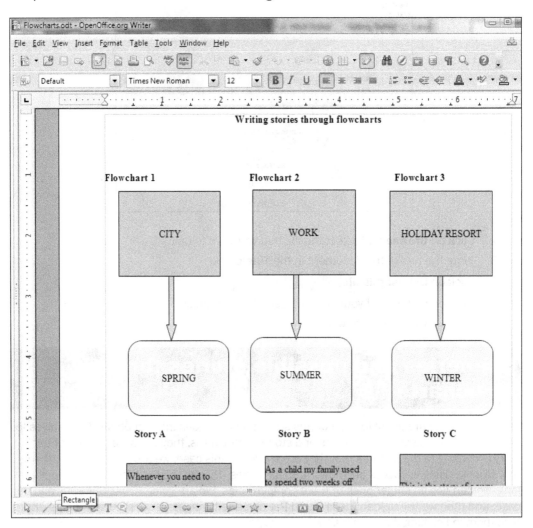

How to do it...

In order to design the previous activity, you must follow these steps:

1. Click on **Add an activity** and choose **Forum**.

2. In the **Forum name** block, write the title of the activity, and in **Forum introduction**, write what the students are going to do, as shown in the following screenshot:

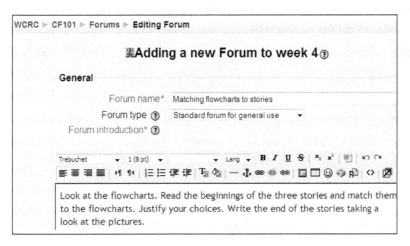

3. Click on **Save and display**.

How it works...

When you see the next screenshot, carry out the following steps:

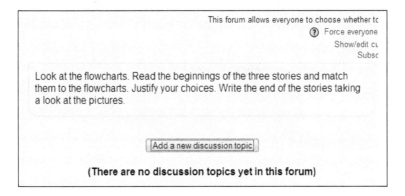

1. Click on **Add a new discussion topic.**

2. The editor appears. Complete the **Subject** block of this editor.

3. Complete the **Message** block with the instructions and repeat the information in the **Forum introduction** as well.

4. Click on **Browse** and upload the document prepared in OpenOffice.

5. Click on **Post to forum**.

6. You have posted the first comment which will be your first activity. It will appear as shown in the next screenshot:

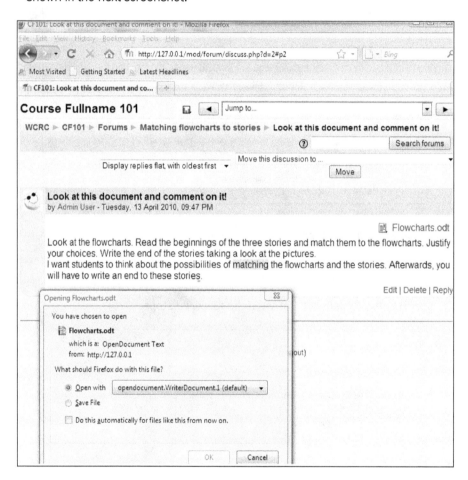

7. Click on **OK** and the document that you have designed will appear as shown in the next screenshot:

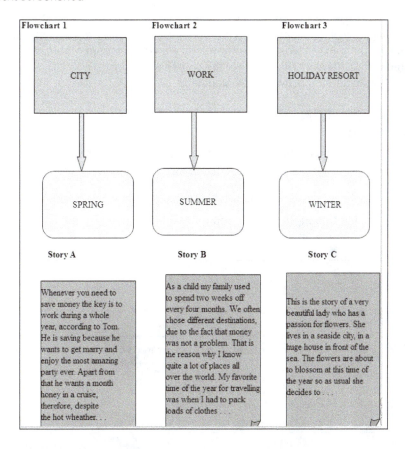

8. Go back to the course.

Working with paintings—Salvador Dali's art

This art is very special, as many things can be perceived from it. Students can read about Salvador Dali's work at: http://en.wikipedia.org/wiki/Salvador_Dal%C3%AD so that they have an idea of his life and work. After visiting the site and getting some knowledge about Salvador Dali, they will visit virtual museums—in this case, the website of the **Museum of Modern Art** (**MoMA**), which is in New York, USA. In both the cases, we will be linking the websites. Later, students are going to focus on The Persistence of Memory—the painting by Salvador Dali that students are going to write about. They are going to imagine that they are inside the picture or animate any inanimate item.

Getting ready

We are going to design the writing activity by using a Workshop. First of all, students are going to read the biography of Salvador Dali. As it is very extensive, they are going to glance through it. After glancing through the biography, they will take a virtual tour of MoMA. We will link the website directly to Dali's painting. We enter the course and select the Weekly outline section in which we want to add the activity. Let's Moodle it!

How to do it...

You are going to design this activity in a Workshop. Click on **Add an activity** and select **Workshop**. Afterwards, you will follow these the steps:

1. Complete the **Submission Title** block by writing the title of the activity.

2. Complete the **Description** block. You will link the websites as shown in the following screenshot:

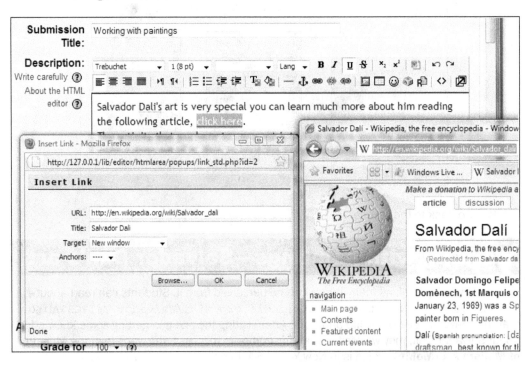

3. In both cases, select **New window** in **Target**, as shown in the following screenshot:

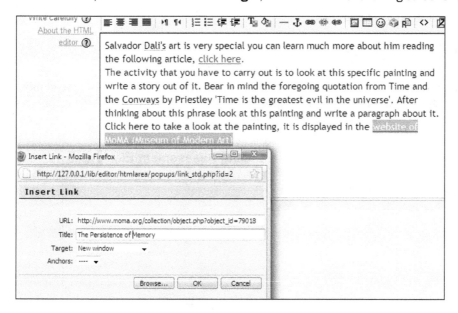

4. There are many items that you can complete according to the way you design the activity. You are going to do it as shown in the next screenshot:

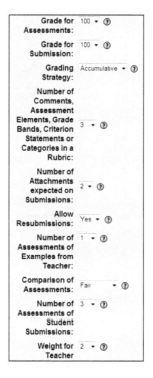

5. Make sure that you check the dates of submissions and assessments.

6. Click on **Save changes**.

How it works...

Now we have to edit assessment elements. In this case, we have chosen three elements, namely, **Grammar**, **Spelling**, and **Composition** (sentences, paragraphs, and so on). We will complete the chart as shown in the next screenshot:

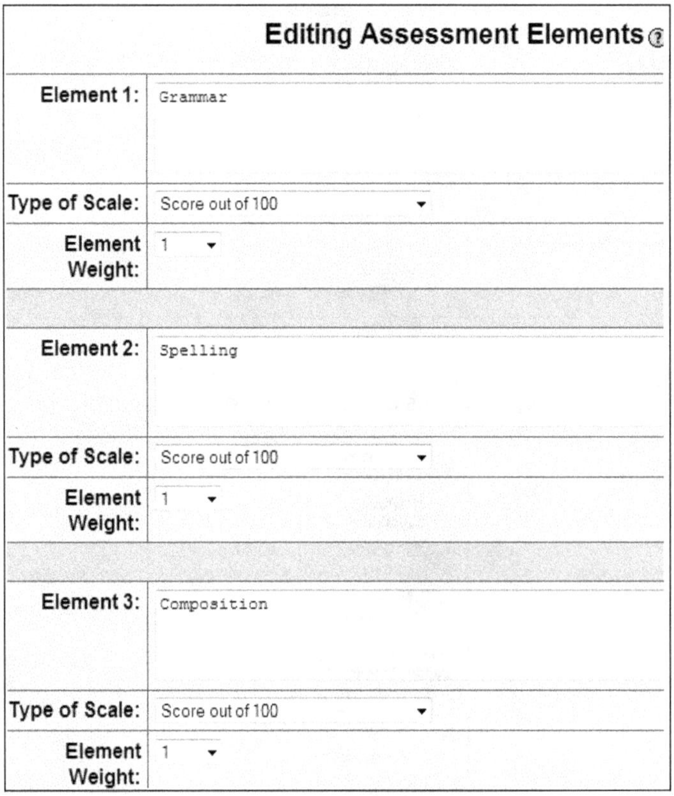

Editing Assessment Elements ⊚	
Element 1:	Grammar
Type of Scale:	Score out of 100 ▾
Element Weight:	1 ▾
Element 2:	Spelling
Type of Scale:	Score out of 100 ▾
Element Weight:	1 ▾
Element 3:	Composition
Type of Scale:	Score out of 100 ▾
Element Weight:	1 ▾

After completing the chart as shown in the previous screenshot, click on **Save changes**. Then click on **Continue**. You can submit an example Assignment so that your students have a sample of writing. Another possibility is that you submit the introduction or some questions to guide their writing.

Choosing a book by its cover

The cover of a book may give the readers an idea about what the book deals with. Usually, we do not judge a book by its cover, but in this case it is a good activity for students to write or predict what the book deals with. It is very difficult to predict whether this book will be our favorite book, or whether we would enjoy this book thoroughly. I think it is interesting to use the title of the book and the picture on the cover to create an activity.

Getting ready

We are going to create a guided writing activity using a Journal, and you can select another activity to carry it out. We are going to design the activity so that our students write a story based on the cover of the book—by taking into account the title and the pictures on its cover. We enter the course and choose the Weekly outline section in which we want to add the activity. Let's Moodle it!

How to do it...

Before creating the activity in Moodle, we have to choose the cover of the book that we will be working on. In this case, we are going to select a book written by Thomas Kinkade, who is a painter as well. The name of the book is *Beyond the Garden Gate*. These are the steps to follow:

1. Click on **Add an activity** and select **Journal**.
2. Complete the **Journal name** and **Journal question**.
3. In the **Journal question**, we are linking the official website of Thomas Kinkade's timeline, `http://www.thomaskinkade.com/magi/servlet/com.asucon.ebiz.biography.web.tk.BiographyServlet` as shown in the following screenshot:

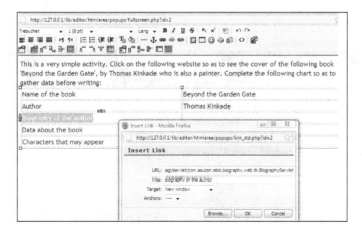

4. You are going to design the table as shown in the previous screenshot. In **Data about the book**, you will be linking the following URL, `http://www.amazon.com/gp/reader/1565075404/ref=sib_dp_pt#reader-link`. Students will be able to preview the book using this website.

5. Make sure that you select **New window** in **Target**.

6. Click **OK**.

7. Then click on **Save and display**.

How it works...

After linking the websites, students can surf these pages and find interesting data about the artist. They can also see his works from an artistic point of view. The link to the official website is very important, as the information is accurate and precise. Now the activity is ready for your students to write! The next screenshot represents the way in which the students will see the activity:

This is a very simple activity. Click on the following website so as to see the cover of the following book 'Beyond the Garden Gate', by Thomas Kinkade who is also a painter. Complete the following chart so as to gather data before writing:

Name of the book	Beyond the Garden Gate
Author	Thomas Kinkade
Biography of the author	
Data about the book	
Characters that may appear	

Read carefully ⑦
Write carefully ⑦
About the HTML editor ⑦

Advising posters

Several types of addictions such as smoking, drugs, and alcohol are widespread among teenagers nowadays. Therefore, in this recipe, it would be interesting for students to design an anti-smoking campaign to avoid future health problems. We can also relate this subject to drugs and alcohol. Unfortunately, these are ordinary addictions among adolescents. There are several websites that advise people against them. What we expect from our students is that they design different advising campaigns after reading several articles and gathering enough information. They are also expected to upload images while designing their anti-smoking campaign and explain the consequences of the addiction. Let's Moodle it!

Getting ready

First of all, we have to surf to select some websites or ask the health instructor in the school for help. We would like our students to research on this topic themselves. It would be interesting and attractive if they have appealing posters, showing how these addictions may prove harmful, especially for teenagers. It would be supportive to supply our students with adequate information so that they gather the data and write an impressive advising campaign.

How to do it...

After selecting the websites that you want your students to work with, you are going to choose the Weekly outline section where you want to introduce the activity. These are the steps you have to follow:

1. Select **Add an activity** and click on **Wiki**.

2. In the **Summary** block, write the title of the activity, in this case **Advising Campaign**.

3. In the **Introduction** block, write the description of the activity that they are going to carry out, as shown in the following screenshot:

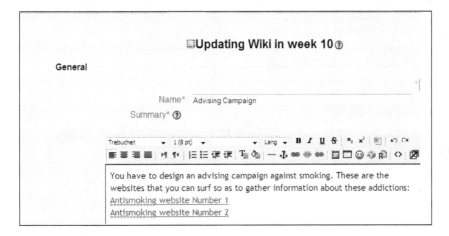

4. After completing the **Introduction** block, you will link the websites. The websites chosen for this activity are as follows: http://www.canberra.edu.au/monitor/articles/new/20080208_anti-smoking and http://kidshealth.org/teen/cancer_center/q_a/quit_smoking.html

5. After linking these websites, select **New window** in **Target**.

6. Click on **Save and return to course**.

How it works...

You have just designed an activity in Moodle. In this case, you asked your students to write an advising campaign through a Wiki so that they can share the data that they have learnt. You can also design this activity through a Forum so that students can share the information or comment on each other's campaign.

Cooking recipes

In this recipe, I suggest that we write a cooking recipe based on the pictures of food shown. It is very difficult to choose a meal that all the students want us to cook, especially if they live in a cosmopolitan city.

Let's choose some vegetables that can be used in different meals. Depending on their preferences, they will be able to write different recipes.

Getting ready

Having used the Journal, carrying out this activity is relatively easy. We will select either the images of some vegetables from clipart or any other free images of vegetables that we can download from the Internet (I have quoted some interesting websites where we can download free images in previous recipes). So we are going to choose the Weekly outline section where we can design the activity. Let's Moodle it!

How to do it...

First of all, choose the clipart of vegetables in Microsoft Word for some recipes that your students could try to cook at home.

An alternate method is selecting some free images from any website, linking the website, or uploading the images by clicking on the icon that inserts the images. After the images are inserted, follow these steps:

1. Click on **Add an activity** and select **Journal**.

2. Complete the **Journal name** block.

3. Then complete the **Journal question** block with the description of the activity, as shown in the following screenshot:

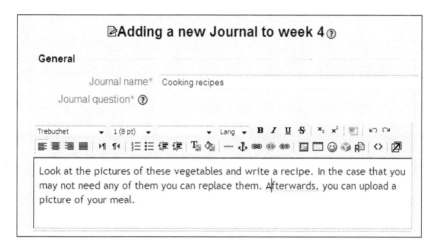

4. Make sure that you upload the clipart from Microsoft Word or link the website depending on your choice.

5. Click on **Save and return to course**.

6. The activity is ready for your students to work on.

How it works...

When your students click on the activity, they will read the title and they can see the pictures that you have uploaded. They can also visit websites containing the pictures of the different vegetables. Afterwards, they are going to write the cooking recipe. They can also express their opinion about their likes and dislikes.

3
Looking at Things from Different Perspectives

When we write, we have to decide the tone and perspective for the piece of writing that we are creating. We have to explain to our students that they may write in first, second, or third person. We know the differences, as they are quite obvious. Therefore, we will ask them to write the pieces of writing in first person. They can do this by imagining that they are one of the characters in the different stories proposed for each recipe.

In this chapter, we are going to insert many techniques for future writers in our Moodle course using a virtual classroom. We will also insert several resources available in Web 2.0, as they should prove attractive to our students. The students are going to carry out the activities along with technology. They will narrate a piece of fiction that already exists from the first person's point of view. They are going to immerse themselves in the story by becoming the character. They can choose any character—either a main character or a secondary one.

In this chapter, we will cover the following topics:

- ▶ How to become a well-known character
- ▶ Understanding secondary characters
- ▶ Adding technology to a story
- ▶ Statues can think
- ▶ Changing an adventure
- ▶ Old age versus childhood
- ▶ Beauty versus ugliness
- ▶ Curious characters

Introduction

In this chapter, you will be able to help your students set their imagination free. You will learn how to apply different techniques to incorporate classical literature by combining Web 2.0 tools, iPod's, iPad's, and iPhone's free software with Moodle. Your students will have to work with eight different books or plays. In case that they have not read them, we will link a website retelling the summary of the story, as they will have to read the entire book to know the plot otherwise. Another possibility is that students read the stories in their iPhones, iPads, or iPods. The books and plays that I propose are classics. So they might have already read them or will be reading them in literature classes.

In this virtual classroom, we are going to enrich the vocabulary of our students and make them read before writing. I always repeat this several times to my students because we learn many things and enhance our vocabulary by reading excellent books. Another important feature to mention is the use of notes and comments on different books or plays. We don't understand everything when reading a book, so we can link to a website that allows us to use free notes on books. They can gather more information to write their activities.

Some of these stories have also been Hollywood successes—so, students can watch the film. This will help them to understand that a book or a story can also be seen from different points of view. This shows how a story changes when it is a film—as in the case of *Romeo and Juliet*. A recent version of *Romeo and Juliet* is set in Miami, and has a mixture of old English and technology, while the main characters are kept in the past.

As stated previously, you can use the ideas and change the stories according to books that your students have read, are reading, or are going to read in the near future. Adding a personal touch to an activity is always productive. I hope that you have read the books or plays that I proposed. If not, you have some homework. Let's Moodle it!

Becoming a well-known character

In this task, we are going to explain to our students the difference between static and dynamic characters. After the difference is explained, we are going to read the book, *The Wonderful Wizard of Oz*, by L. Frank Baum. In this book, most of the main characters are dynamic except for the dog Toto. We are going to ask our students to be one of the developing characters in *The Wonderful Wizard of Oz*. The students will add changes to the story by imagining that they belong in the book. I propose to do this task through Moodle and by using Web 2.0. This is done by creating many links to get enough information in case the students have not read the book yet.

Getting ready

Let's ask our students to write an essay by imagining that they are one dynamic character in *The Wonderful Wizard of Oz*. First of all, we will tell them the difference between static and dynamic characters. We will create a link to the website. When they have to write the essay, we will be linking to another website where they can find the necessary information about the book. We are going to carry out this activity in Quiz using the Essay option. Let's Moodle it!

How to do it...

Enter the course and select the Weekly outline section in which you want to add the activity. Then follow these steps:

1. Click on the drop-down box in **Add an activity** and select **Quiz**.

2. In the **Name** block, write the title of the Quiz, and in **Introduction**, link to a website in which students can find the difference between dynamic and static characters as shown in the following screenshot:

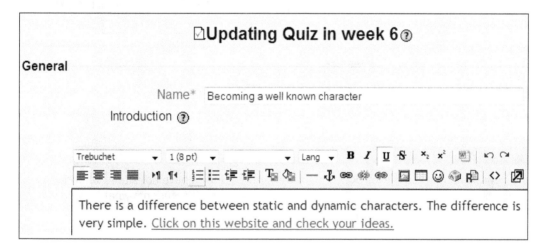

3. The website that you will be linking to is shown in the next screenshot: `http://www.cliffsnotes.com/WileyCDA/Section/What-is-a-dynamic-character-What-is-a-static-character-How-are-they-different-.id-305408,articleId-7986.html`.

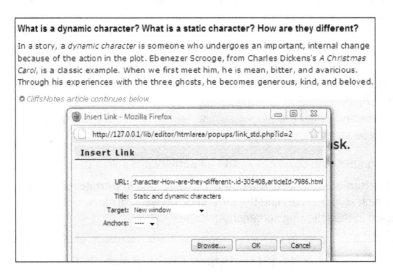

4. In **Target**, select **New window**.

5. You can complete the other items in this activity.

6. Now, click on **Save and display**.

How it works...

We have so far created the introduction for the activity. But we have not stated what our students have to do. So, we design the essay and explain to the students what they have to do. You have to follow these steps:

1. Click on the drop-down box and select **Create a new question**. Then select **Essay**.

2. In the **Question name**, write the title of the essay—**Becoming a well known character**.

3. In **Question text**, you can give information about the story of **The Wonderful Wizard of Oz**. In this case, you will link to Wikipedia, and to a webpage where the students can read the book if they haven't read it. This is shown in the following screenshot:

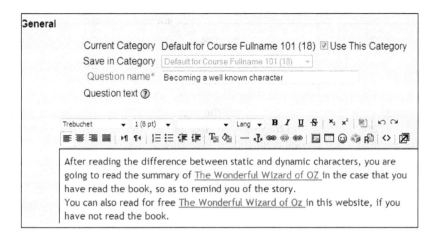

4. The URLs of the websites are as follows:

    ❏ `http://en.wikipedia.org/wiki/The_Wonderful_Wizard_Of_Oz.`

    ❏ `http://www.gutenberg.org/files/55/55-h/55-h.htm.`

5. In the **General feedback** block, write the title of the essay and explain to your students what they have to do, as shown in the following screenshot:

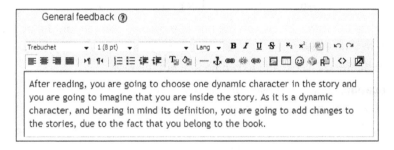

6. Click on **Save changes**.

7. Check the activity that you have already created and then click on **Add to quiz**.

8. Click on **Go**.

9. Go back to the course.

Understanding secondary characters

We are going to design a reading comprehension and writing activity. Students are going to read the play *Romeo and Juliet* by William Shakespeare. This play is a tragedy due to the mistake of a secondary character—the Friar who has the idea to prepare the magic poison to put Juliet to sleep for 42 hours, but miscarries the message to Romeo. Students are going to imagine that they are the Friar and they have to change the advice. What advice would the students give to Juliet when she asks for help if they were in the Friar's shoes?

We are going to do this activity by adding resources to the course separately. After adding the resources, we are going to create a Journal. In this Journal, our students have to write the advice they would give to Juliet. In addition to this, we can also create an **Online text** activity. Let's Moodle it!

Getting ready

We are going to work with the tragedy of *Romeo and Juliet*. We are going to add two links to the websites in the **Add a resource** option. First, we will link to a website where students can read the play in case that they haven't already. Then we will link to another website, the analysis of Friar Lawrence. Our students will imagine that they are Friar Lawrence in the activity. These are the steps that you have to follow:

1. Click on **Add a resource** and select **Link to a file or web site**.

2. Complete the **Name** block with the title of the book—**Romeo and Juliet play by William Shakespeare**.

3. In the **Summary** block, add a comment about the play.

4. In **Location**, copy the website URL. In this case, it is:
   `http://www.gutenberg.org/dirs/etext98/2ws1610.txt`.

5. In the **Window** block, select **New window** as shown in the following screenshot:

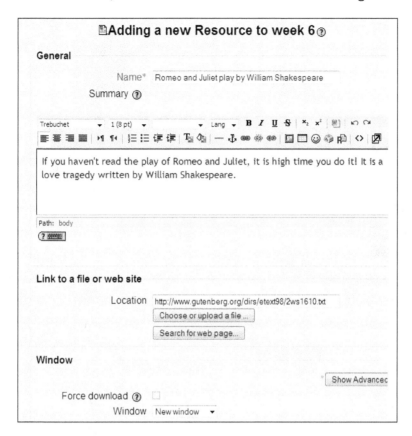

6. Click on **Save and return to course**.

How to do it...

We have just created the link to the tragic play by William Shakespeare. Now we are going to create another link to a website. Our students can just read the description of the Friar Lawrence character. Let's do the same as in the prior explanation but change the URL. So let's do it!

1. Click on **Add a resource** and select **Link to a file or web site**.

2. Complete the **Name** block with what the students are going to deal with, **Character analysis Friar Lawrence**.

3. In **Location**, copy the website URL. In this case:

```
http://www.cliffsnotes.com/WileyCDA/LitNote/Romeo-and-Juliet-
Character-Analysis-Friar-Laurence.id-165,pageNum-267.html.
```

4. In the **Window** block, select **New window** as shown in the following screenshot:

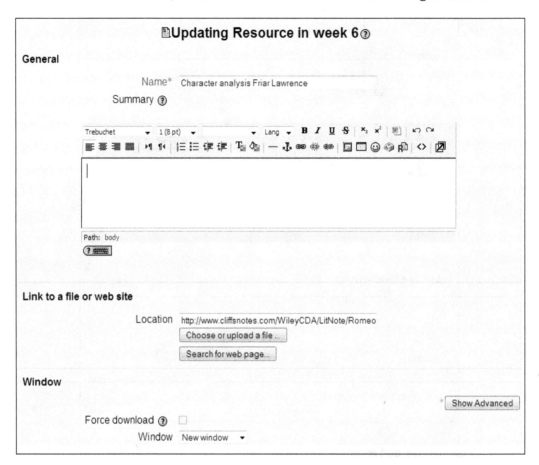

5. Click on **Save and return to course**.

How it works...

After linking the two websites as resources, we are going to create the activity that our students have to carry out, which is writing the advice that they would give Juliet so as to change the play. We are going to do it in a Journal, which is a very simple activity, though you can also carry out the activity in **Online text** within Assignments. We select this option because students only have to offer their advice here. You have to follow these steps:

1. Click on **Add an activity** and select **Journal**.

2. Complete the **Journal name** block with the title of the activity.

3. Complete the **Journal question** expanding the explanation of the title as shown in the following screenshot:

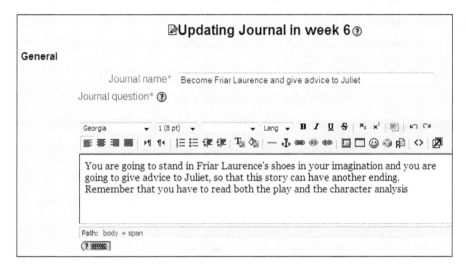

4. Click on **Save and return to course**.

There's more...

We have created three activities for our students. We have created two reading comprehension activities and a writing activity. Now we can create a glossary.

Creating a glossary with the characters

Instead of using a glossary in the traditional way, we are going to develop one in which our students list all the characters in the play and give some information about each character. They do not need to write tons of information, only the most important facts regarding each character. You must be wondering about how this can be done. It is quite simple. Let's create a glossary. Follow these steps:

1. Click on **Add an activity** and select **Glossary**.

2. In the **Name** block, write the title.

3. In the **Description** block, write what the students have to do, as shown in the following screenshot:

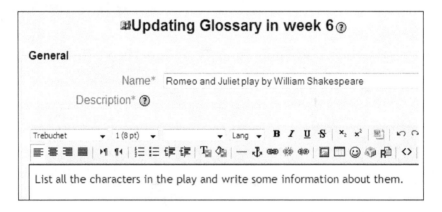

4. Click on **Save and return to course**.

Creating a crossword using the Glossary

After students have created a glossary using the description of the characters in *Romeo and Juliet*, you can create a crossword to test their knowledge. Students love doing such quizzes. You can create a crossword from Hot Potatoes by following these steps:

1. Open Hot Potatoes and click on **JCross**—the red potato.

2. Add a title to the crossword.

3. Click on **Manage Grid** and select **Automatic Grid-maker**.

4. Enter words in the block that appears, as shown in the following screenshot:

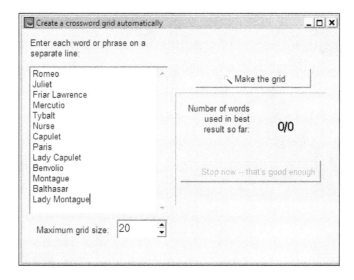

5. Click on **Make the grid**.

6. Click on **Add Clues** and add the clues to the crossword.

7. After adding the clues, click on **OK**.

8. Click on **File**, select **Save As**, and name your file.

9. Click on **Save**.

Uploading the crossword to Moodle

We are going to upload the crossword puzzle to Moodle. It is quite simple. Follow these steps:

1. Click on **Add an activity** and select **Hot Potatoes Quiz**.

2. Click on **Choose or upload a file**.

3. Click on **Upload a file**.

4. Click on **Browse** and search for your crossword.

5. When you find the file, click on **Open**.

6. Click on **Upload this file** as shown in the following screenshot:

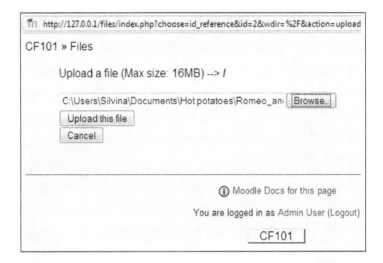

7. Click on the file.
8. After the file is uploaded, click on **Save and return to course**.
9. The crossword is ready to work!

Adding technology to a story

In this recipe, we are going to add technology to the story of *Hansel and Gretel*. We are going to ask our students to imagine that both Hansel and Gretel have a cell phone. If the student is a girl, she is going to play Gretel. On the other hand, if the student is a boy, he is going to play Hansel. What happens when they find the person inside the chocolate house? We are going to create a link to a website from where they can read the story of *Hansel and Gretel*. After reading this story, the students can use a Forum to brainstorm ideas among themselves and to upload images. Later, they can write a different plot and end to this story in a Journal, using their ideas. Let's Moodle it!

Getting ready

We are going to create an activity where the students can change the story. First of all, we will create a link to a website where they can read the story so that they can enhance their vocabulary as well. I really find this website quite interesting. Afterwards, we can add a picture of Hansel and Gretel eating chocolate in the special house. We are going to create a document in Microsoft Word and insert an image of Hansel and Gretel with cell phones in their hands. We will give a name to the document and then save it. We will use this document later. So let's Moodle it!

How to do it...

We will enter the course and select the Weekly outline section where we want to add this activity so that we can design it. These are the steps to follow:

1. Click on **Add an activity** and select **Forum**.

2. In the **Forum name** block, write the title of the activity.

3. In the **Forum introduction** block, broaden the title of the activity. You are also going to create the link to the website as shown in the following screenshot:

4. Complete the **Insert Link** block as shown in the previous screenshot.

5. Click on **OK**.

6. Click on **Save and display**.

7. Click on **Add a new discussion topic** and write about the first discussion topic and picture as shown in the following screenshot:

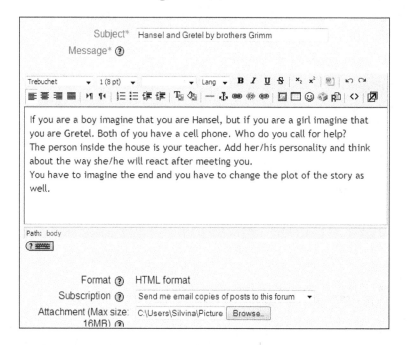

8. Click on **Browse** and look for the file that you have created in Microsoft Word with the picture of Hansel, Gretel, and the chocolate house.

9. After the file is found, select it and click on **Post to forum**.

10. Click on **Continue**.

11. Go back to the course.

How it works...

The teacher gives the first tip so that the students start brainstorming. After brainstorming ideas through a Forum, students have enough elements to write a new story. The idea is that they gather data and combine them together. In other words, they can write a beautiful piece of writing instead of watching the screen without knowing which letter to press. Although this activity can be carried out in **Online text** within Assignments, we are going to create a Journal activity so that the students can write their stories themselves. Create a Journal activity by following these steps:

1. Click on **Add an activity** and select **Journal**.

2. Complete the **Journal name** with the title of the activity.

3. Complete the **Journal question** with the instructions that the students have to follow as shown in the following screenshot:

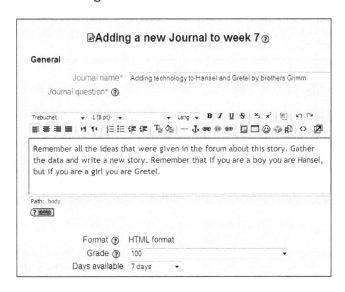

4. Click on **Save and return to course**.

Statues can think

In this recipe, we are going to develop a reading comprehension and a writing activity. The writing activity will be connecting the differences in the thinking of our students. We are going to develop this activity in Wiki. The story that they are going to read is *The Legend of King Midas*, who was an extremely greedy man. Accidentally, his daughter becomes a statue. He became wiser after this incident and learned that money is not everything in the world. So, we are going to concentrate on the part in which his daughter turns into a statue. We will ask our students to think from the statue's point of view.

Getting ready

We are going to design a Wiki activity. First of all, we are going to select the website that our students are going to read before writing. After the website is selected, we will enter the course and choose the Weekly outline section in which we want to add the activity. Let's Moodle it!

How to do it...

You are going to follow these steps in order to design the activity previously introduced.

1. Click on **Add an activity** and select **Wiki**.

2. In the **Name** block, write the title of the activity.

3. In the **Summary block**, write about what the students have to do. We will also add a link to the website as shown in the following screenshot:

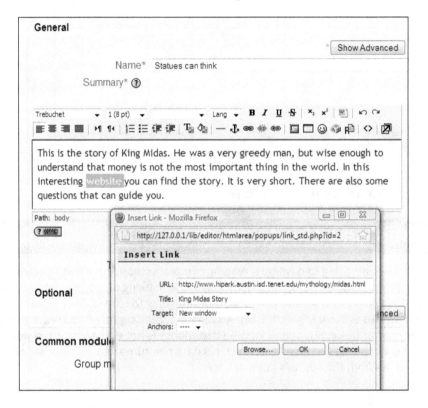

4. To link to a website, highlight the word **website** and click on the chain icon.

5. In **Target**, select **New window**.

6. Click on **OK**.

7. Click on **Save and return to course**.

How it works...

Students should read the story of King Midas before doing the activity. When students click on the activity, it appears as shown in the next screenshot:

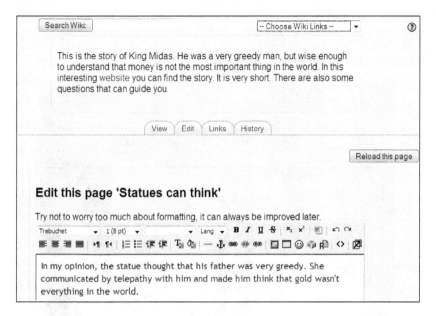

If students click on **Edit**, they can change the input from other students. They can write the answers to the questions mentioned previously. They can also open that website in a new window as we have done previously so that they do not have to close the activity.

Changing an adventure

Reading is very important because our students obtain a lot of vocabulary from this passive activity. There are several 'musts' in real or virtual bookcases. These books can help our students set their imagination free, and they can find a lot of interesting words to improve their vocabulary when writing. Can you guess which book I am going to propose for the following activity in Moodle? Have a look in the following bookcase. The book is available as shown in the following screenshot:

(Image credit: `http://www.ivyjoy.com/bookmark.htm`)

Getting ready

Yes! That is the book. *Alice in Wonderland* by Lewis Carroll. We are going to design a writing activity through an **Online text**, a type of Assignment activity. First of all, we are going to create a link to a file where students can read the book. Afterwards, they are going to change the adventure of Alice. She is not going to follow the white rabbit, as she will prepare a campsite in the forest. So the story will change its course and students will have to write from Alice's point of view. We enter the course and choose the Weekly outline section in which we want to add the activity. Let's Moodle it!

How to do it...

First of all, we will create create a link to the website where the students can read the book *Alice in Wonderland*. You may ask them to read only the first chapter and then write the end of the story. You will follow these steps:

1. Complete the **Name** block by writing the name of the book.

2. Complete the **Link to a file or website** block with the following URL:
   `http://www.ivyjoy.com/fables/aliceintro.html`.

3. Choose **New window** in the **Window** block, as shown in the following screenshot:

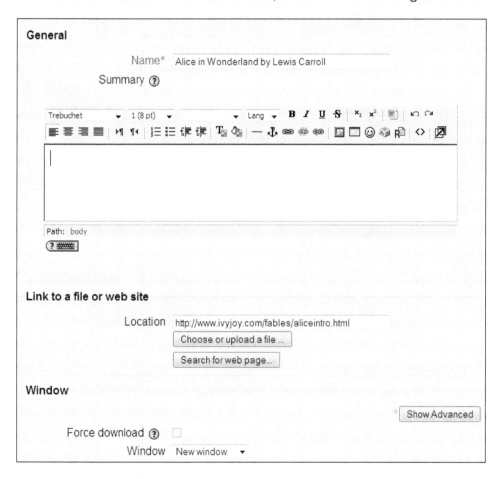

4. Click on **Save and return to course**.

How it works...

We have to write the activity. This time we are going to carry out the activity in **Online text**—an option in Moodle's Assignment module. We are going to ask our students to be in Alice's shoes and change the course of the story. We are going to tell them that Alice decides to camp in the forest instead of following the white rabbit. These are the steps to follow:

1. Click on **Add an activity**.

2. Choose **Online text**.

3. Write a title in the **Assignment name** block.

4. Complete the **Description** block by elaborating on the title and explain to the students what they have to do as shown in the following screenshot:

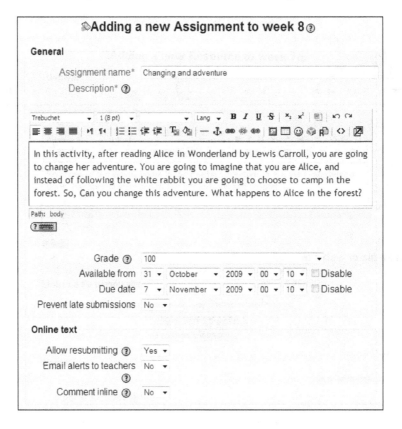

5. **Grade** the students based on their performance in these activities.

6. You may change the following options based on the way you want to focus your activity.

7. Click on **Save and return to course**.

There's more...

We saw how to create a link to a website where students can read a book. Now we will see how to create a link to a site where students can listen to the book.

Linking to a website where students can listen to Alice in Wonderland

You will see how the page allows you to listen to the book instead of reading it. You can add a resource using both websites—one where they can read the book and another where they can listen to it. Maybe they like to listen as they read the story. In such a case, you can combine both the websites. This can be done by following these steps:

1. Click on **Add a resource** and select **Link to a file or web site**.

2. Complete the **Name** block by writing the name of the book and add the words **Listen to**.

3. Complete the **Summary** block with additional information that you want to give to your students, as shown in the following screenshot:

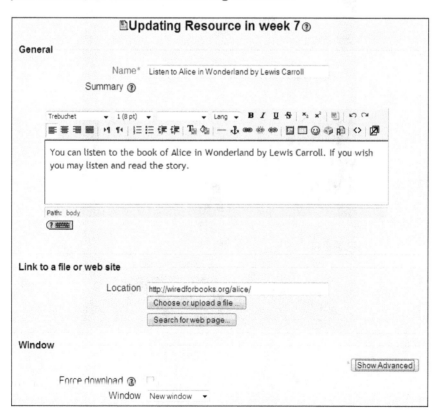

4. In the **Link to a file or web site** block, write the URL that you are going to use.

5. In the **Window** block, select **New window**.

6. Click on **Save and return to course**.

Reading Alice in Wonderland in your iPod touch, iPad, or iPhone

You can also read this story using an iPod touch, iPad, or iPhone if you or your students happen to have one of them. You have to install Classics2GoCollection (Free version), which includes *Alice in Wonderland* by Lewis Carroll and an e-book reader. It is developed by KiwiTech. The website URL where you can find more information is: `http://www.classics2goapp.com/index.html`.

It is shown in the next screenshots:

Old age versus childhood

Let's ask our students to imagine themselves as an old man, and then change the attitude of a character in a story. Students should imagine that they are Santiago—an old man in the story, *The Old Man and the Sea*, by Ernest Hemingway. What would they do instead of catching a great fish? What if the old man decides to sail for adventures instead?

Getting ready

We will design a writing activity in which we will give students the beginning for a story. After the students read the summary of the story in which the end is not disclosed, they are going to write an alternate end to it. We will create a link to the website. After we link the website, students will write the end. We enter the course and choose the Weekly outline section in which we want to add the activity. Let's Moodle it!

How to do it...

In this case, we are going to use a different option in the Assignments activity module. We are going to ask our students to upload a single file. In this file, they have to include the picture of an old man changing his adventure. He has to be well rested before he starts his journey on the boat. Let's wait and see what they imagine. These are the steps to follow:

1. Click on **Add an activity** and select **Upload a single file**.

2. Complete the **Assignment name** block. Write the title of the activity.

3. Complete the **Description** block. After completing the description block, create two links to the websites.

4. One of the links is the summary of part one—it does not tell us the end. The URL of the website is as follows: `http://www.cliffsnotes.com/WileyCDA/LitNote/The-Old-Man-and-the-Sea-Summary-and-Analysis-by-Chapter-Part-One-Preparations.id-102,pageNum-11.html`.

5. The other link is the Character Map, and the URL of the website is: `http://www.cliffsnotes.com/WileyCDA/LitNote/The-Old-Man-and-the-Sea-Character-Map.id-102,pageNum-74.html`.

6. In both cases, the links to the websites are in **New window** when completing the **Target** block as shown in the following screenshot:

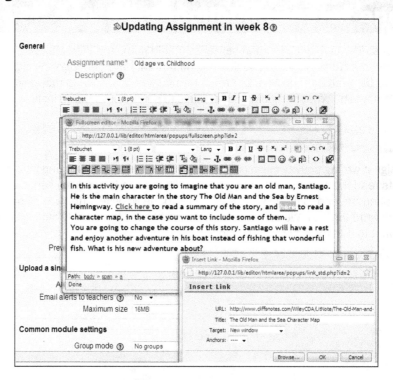

7. Complete the other blocks in the way you want your students to design the activity.

8. Click on **Save and return to course**.

How it works...

After designing the activity, you may switch roles with students and carry out the activity yourself. When you click on the activity, what appears is shown in the next screenshot:

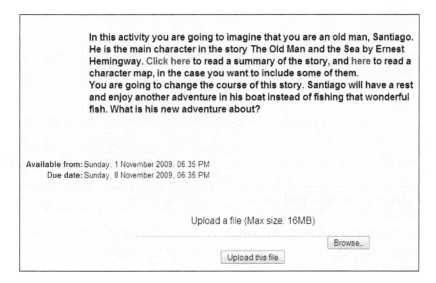

In this activity you are going to imagine that you are an old man, Santiago. He is the main character in the story The Old Man and the Sea by Ernest Hemingway. Click here to read a summary of the story, and here to read a character map, in the case you want to include some of them.
You are going to change the course of this story. Santiago will have a rest and enjoy another adventure in his boat instead of fishing that wonderful fish. What is his new adventure about?

Available from: Sunday, 1 November 2009, 06.35 PM
Due date: Sunday, 8 November 2009, 06:35 PM

Upload a file (Max size: 16MB)

Browse..

Upload this file

Your students will edit the file by using another software, which is not part of the Moodle package. They are to prepare the file offline and afterwards they are going to upload it. They can insert images in the writing—each student has his or her own style when presenting this activity. It is quite interesting to give the students this kind of freedom from time to time, especially when writing.

Beauty versus ugliness

In this recipe, we are going to ask our students to discuss the topic in the title. How important is beauty for our students? Are they aware of the fact that beauty isn't everything? Do they know that the internal beauty of a person is the most important aspect to be considered? Let's wait and read what they have to tell us. We are going to ask our students to read *The Phantom of the Opera* by Gaston Leroux. After they have read it, we are going to use the chat option in Moodle so that they can discuss this topic, which is linked to the story that they have read. Then, they have to write a different ending to the story of *The Phantom of the Opera* taking on different roles irrespective of gender, imagining that they are either Christine Daae or The Phantom. Let's Moodle it!

Getting ready

We are going to create a chat in Moodle so that our students can discuss the topic of external beauty versus ugliness. Then we are going to add a resource by linking to a website. In this website, they can read the story of *The Phantom of the Opera*. Next, taking into account the discussion and the story that they have read, they are going to write a different end to this story by taking on roles irrespective of their gender.

How to do it...

First of all, you are going to choose the Weekly outline section where you want to create the activity. Then you are going to follow these steps:

1. Select **Add an activity** and click on **Chat.**

2. Complete the **Name of this chat room** block, writing the title of the discussion.

3. Complete the **Introduction text**, elaborating the title of the discussion.

4. In the **Save past sessions** block, select the option **Never delete messages.** This is done so that everyone can double check what they wrote for their essay.

5. In **Everyone can view past sessions**, select **Yes** for the same reason as the previous one.

6. Complete the blocks as shown in the following screenshot:

7. Click on **Save and return to course.**

How it works...

The activity is half done as we have created the interactive part of it. However, the link to the website where they can read the book is missing! So we are going to create a link to the place where they can read it. These are the steps that you need to follow:

1. Click on **Add a resource** and select **Link to a file or a web site**.

2. Complete the **Name** block—write the title of the book and its author.

3. Complete the **Summary** block, you can write the description of the book.

4. Write the URL in the **Location** block.

5. In the **Window** block, choose **New window**, as shown in the next screenshot:

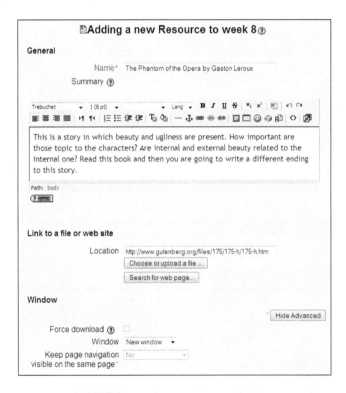

6. Click on **Save and return to course**.

There's more...

We have already created an interactive activity and a passive one. Now it is high time for our students to concentrate on writing. Let's allow them to become another character and stand in somebody else's shoes again.

Creating a writing activity after chatting and reading

In this task, students have to write a different end to the story. So let's create the writing activity in our Moodle course. Follow these steps:

1. Click on **Add an activity** and select **Advanced uploading of files** within Assignments.
2. Complete the **Assignment name** block with the title of the activity.
3. Complete the **Description** block, writing what they have to do.
4. Complete the following blocks as shown in the next screenshot:

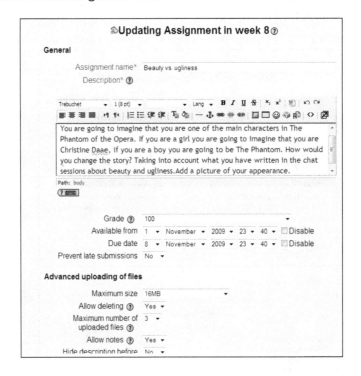

5. Click on **Save and return to course**.

The activity is ready to work with.

Curious characters

In this recipe, I suggest that we write by taking into account the personality of the students. Though a student has to be the main character in *The Secret Garden* by Frances Hodgson Burnett, he or she should say whether or not they would act the way the female lead did. They would change the name of the story if they do not care about plants or nature. So why don't we find more about the interest of our students through their writing. Let's Moodle it!

Getting ready

We have already used the Journal, though you can select **Online text**, as this is a very simple activity. We will choose a link to a website where students can either get information or read the book. We can also select an article on Wikipedia, summarizing the story or the book. In this case, we are going to create a link to the complete book. The title of the book tells us something, since as readers we already know that there exists a secret garden somewhere. So we are going to select the Weekly outline section in which we want to design the activity.

How to do it...

We are going to create a link to the website where we want our students to read the book, and afterwards we are going to tell them what they have to do. So these are the steps that you have to follow:

1. Click on **Add a resource** and select **Link to a file or web site**.

2. Complete the **Name** block, writing the name of the book.

3. Complete the **Summary** block with more information that you want to give to your students, as shown in the next screenshot:

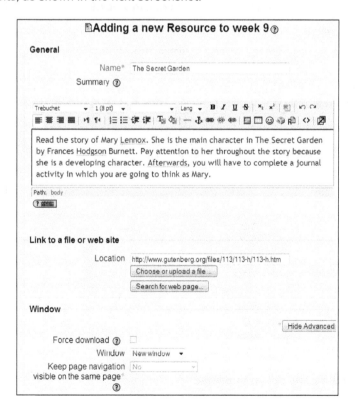

4. In the **Link to a file or web site** block, write the URL that you are going to work with.

5. In the **Window** block, select **New window**.

6. Click on **Save and return to course**.

How it works...

After creating the link to the website, we are going to create the writing activity in which the students have to write how they would behave if they were Mary Lennox. Would they be as curious as she was? We are going to focus on finding the garden and the way she behaves throughout the story. Although this book contains a dramatic story, if we focus on finding the garden and how the character evolves, it could be fascinating. You can also suggest to your students that they watch the movie. These are the steps that you have to follow:

1. Click on **Add an activity** and select **Journal**.

2. Complete the **Journal name** block with the title of the activity.

3. Complete the **Journal question** expanding the explanation of the title, as shown in the following screenshot:

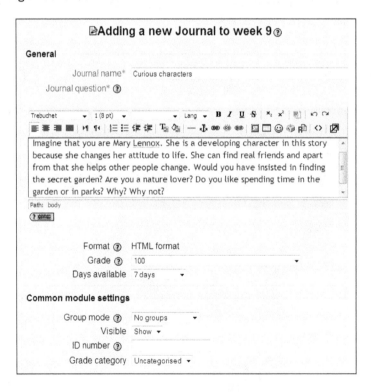

4. Click on **Save and return to course**.

4
Defining Types of Sentences

We will introduce the students to different types of sentences. They are going to practice on each type of sentence using different approaches. First, they are going to practice on each type individually. After our students complete this Exercise, we will mix all the sentences. This will help our students to identify and use these sentences properly. We will design different types of Exercises such as multiple choice questions, mixing paragraphs, puzzle sentences, and the comparison of a composition to a hamburger. All these Exercises will help our students to write proper paragraphs. In addition to these Exercises, we will also use as many resources as possible from Web 2.0 and Moodle 1.9.5.

In this chapter, we will cover:

- ▶ Embedding videos, games, and matching the correct topic sentence
- ▶ Writing detailed sentences according to the topic sentence
- ▶ Multiple choice questions—selecting the correct concluding sentence
- ▶ Mixing paragraphs
- ▶ Selecting correct sentences
- ▶ Adding detailed sentences
- ▶ Writing the topic and the concluding sentences
- ▶ Hamburger paragraph—writing a composition using three types of sentences

Introduction

In this chapter, you will be designing several types of Exercises concerning reading comprehension and writing and composing through Moodle. Using Moodle we can embed videos from TeacherTube and design games. It also allows us to use multiple choice questions, and provides elements to compare a piece of writing to something that they are familiar with—such as a hamburger, while completing the Moodle courses. Apart from that, hints will be provided on how to develop the same activity in another way by using resources from Web 2.0.

In this virtual classroom, we are going to help our students with the usage of different types of sentences. First, we will introduce them to a sentence and then we will explain their different types. After the explanation, the students will start solving the matching Exercises as practice. Once the matching Exercise is completed, they will supply the descriptive sentences and form a piece of writing that involves the three types of sentences in addition to a title. We are going to work in such a way that these eight recipes will help them to learn and use the sentences correctly, as they will be practiced beforehand in a simpler way.

As stated in the earlier chapters, activities are designed in such a way that the level of difficulty increases as you get further into the book, and the level of challenge for student writing also increases. In this chapter, we are going to focus on writing, which is an active and productive skill. However, some of the Exercises involve reading comprehension, as it is necessary for matching or choosing the correct sentences.

As mentioned previously, I hope that you enjoy the activities. You can also add a personal touch to any recipe. Let's Moodle it!

Embedding videos, games, and matching the correct topic sentence

In this task, we are going to embed a video from `http://www.teachertube.com` about different types of sentences. After the embedding, we are going to link to a website that explains what a topic sentence is. Then we are going to design a game and create a link to its webpage. After the linking, students will select one of the topics of the game and write a paragraph about it. There is no need to panic as it is quite simple. We will just use as many resources as possible to enhance our Moodle course.

The students will watch the video about types of sentences. After watching it, they will read the definition of a topic sentence and its uses. Both activities are passive, so let's add a resource for these two activities.

Getting ready

Enter the course and choose the Weekly outline section where you want to add the activity. First of all, you have to check whether the multimedia filter is available to embed the video. Then embed the video from `http://www.teachertube.com`, which explains the different types of sentences. Follow these steps:

1. Click on **Add a resource** and select **Compose a webpage**.

2. Complete the **Name** block.

3. Complete the **Summary** block.

4. Complete the **Compose a web page** block.

5. Click on the **Toggle HTML Source** icon that has these symbols: **<>**.

6. The URL of the webpage that you want to embed is: `http://www.teachertube.com/viewVideo.php?video_id=132153&title=Four_Types_of_Sentences`.

7. Go to that website and copy the **Embeddable Player** as shown in the next screenshot:

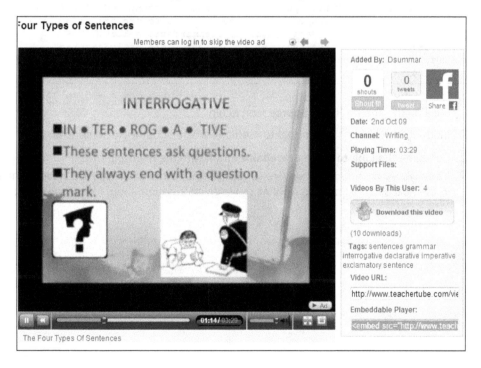

8. Paste the **Embeddable Player** in the **Compose a web page** block. This will appear as shown in the following screenshot:

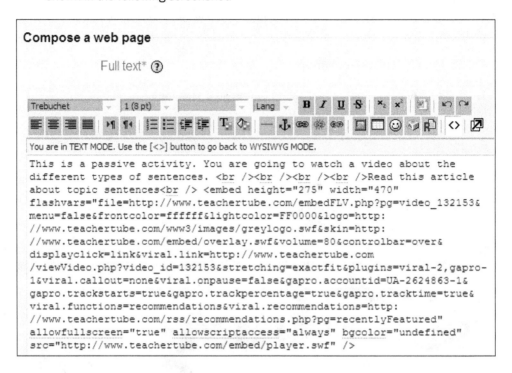

9. Click on the **Toggle HTML Source** icon again.

10. Instruct the students (in writing) to read the article about topic sentences.

11. Complete the **Link to a file or website** block with the following URL:
    `http://www2.actden.com/writ_Den/Tips/paragrap/topic.htm` as shown in the next screenshot. This website provides information about topic sentences:

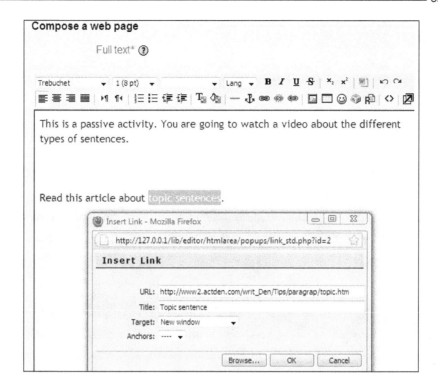

12. In the **Target** block, select **New window**.

13. Click on **Save and display**. This activity is displayed in the next screenshot:

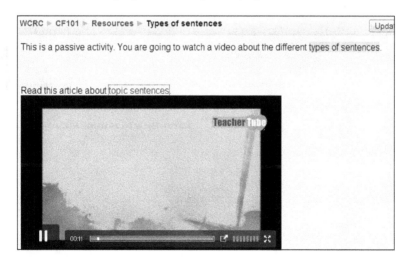

14. Students click on the video to watch it, and later they click on **Types of sentences** and read about topic sentences.

How to do it...

Go to `http://www.what2learn.com/`, to create a game. Students have to read different short paragraphs and they will have to select the correct beginning for each topic sentence. Follow these steps to create the game:

1. Click on **Make a game**.

2. Choose **3D Quiz Maze**.

3. Click on **Next**.

4. Click on **Make a game**.

5. Complete the eight blocks with different paragraphs and the choice of the topic sentences, as shown in the following screenshot:

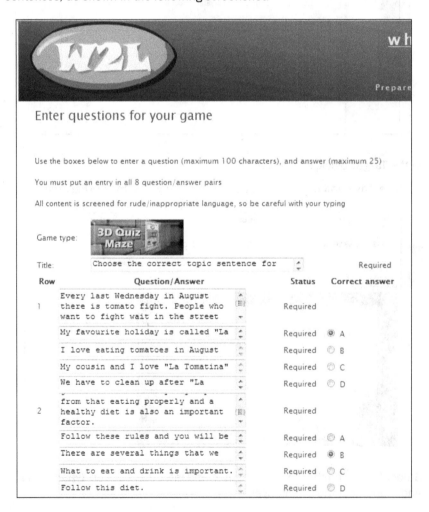

6. Select the correct sentence by clicking on the correct radio button as shown previously.

7. In **Add a tag to your game**, select **English**, as shown in the next screenshot:

8. Click on **Confirm questions**.

9. Click on **Create a game**.

10. Click on **Play your new game**.

11. Select the maze that you want to, as shown in the following screenshot:

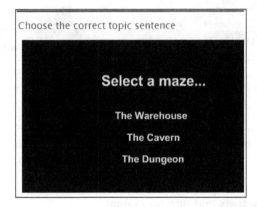

12. The game is ready to be played. Try it yourself! The backdrop of the game appears as shown in the following screenshot:

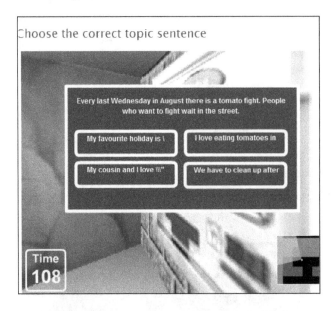

Choose the correct topic sentence

Every last Wednesday in August there is a tomato fight. People who want to fight wait in the street.

My favourite holiday is \

I love eating tomatoes in

My cousin and I love \\\"

We have to clean up after

Time
108

How it works...

After designing the game, the next step is to insert the game into Moodle. We need to create a link to the page and therefore we are going to create a link to the website using a Journal. You can also carry out the activity in **Online text** in Assignments. We want our students to write after they have played the game. Follow these steps:

1. Select **Add an activity** and click on **Journal.**

2. Complete the **Journal name.**

3. Complete the **Journal question.**

4. Create a link to the website where you create the game as shown in the following screenshot:

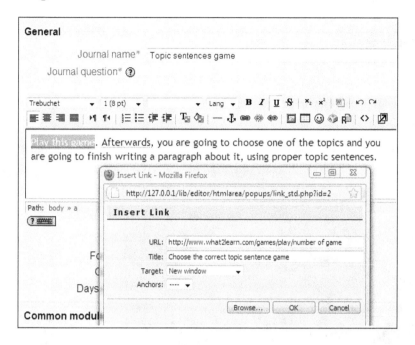

5. Complete the **Insert Link** block.

6. In the **URL** block, if it says **number of game**, then it will show the number of games that you have created.

7. In the **Target** block, select **New window**.

8. Click on **OK**.

9. Click on **Save and return to course**.

There's more

We have created several activities in this recipe. We have embedded a video from TeacherTube and we have designed a multiple choice activity in a game. We have created a link to a website in order to upload that game in our Moodle course, but an alternate option is to embed that game. Embedding is better than linking to a website because of privacy and security issues.

Embedding the game

You can also embed the game instead of linking to a website. In order to do this, follow these steps:

1. Select **Add an activity** and click on **Journal**.
2. Complete the **Journal name**.
3. Complete the **Journal question**.
4. Click on the **Toggle HTML Source** icon, which has these symbols: **<>**.
5. Go to the webpage where you want your game to be embedded.
6. Go to that website and copy the **Embed**—either small, medium, or large as shown in the following screenshot:

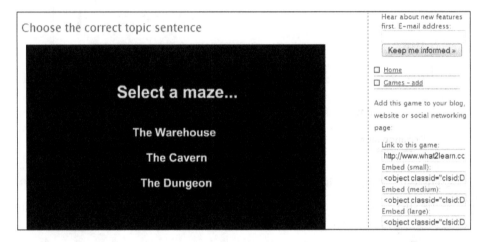

7. Paste the game which you have already selected.
8. Click again on the **<>** icon.
9. Click on **Save and return to course**.

The game is now embedded and ready to be played.

Writing detailed sentences according to the topic sentence

Using this recipe, you can design a reading comprehension activity about different types of sentences. We will link to a website of the different types of sentences, especially detailed sentences. The website is interesting as well as appealing because of the images. Students should read this article, which gives them tips on how to write detailed sentences. After going through this article, they are to write detailed sentences about a topic. You can choose another website. Let's Moodle it!

Getting ready

As mentioned previously, I have selected a website for students to read an article about types of sentences. We are going to ask our students to carry out this activity by uploading a file. The reason is very simple: they may also add images easily by using any word processor.

How to do it...

We are going to select the Weekly outline section where we want to add the activity. Then we are going to follow these steps:

1. Select **Add an activity**, and within **Assignments**, select **Upload a single file**.

2. Complete the **Assignment name** block.

3. Complete the **Description** block in which you are going to create the link to the website, as shown in the following screenshot:

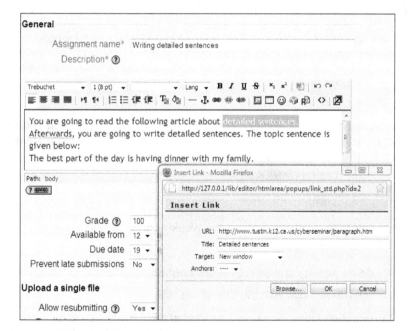

4. Complete the **Insert Link** block, and in **Target**, choose **New window**.

5. Click on **OK**.

6. Click on **Save and return to course**.

How it works...

Students are going to click on the activity and they are going to read the article about detailed sentences. This article also gives them tips on how to write. It will be very easy for them to do the homework. They may also add pictures to the sentences, (as some students add stickers to the pages).

Multiple choice: choose the correct concluding sentence

In this recipe, we are going to create a "multiple choice" Exercise. We are going to present students with a paragraph and they will select the correct concluding sentence. We are going to create a link to a website where they can find some information about concluding sentences. There are also activities concerning the selection of the correct sentence. We will create an alternate link that will contain the description of the place that the students have to read about.

The students are also going to imagine that they can go to this place for a holiday and can write their experience afterwards. Let's Moodle it!

Getting ready

We will create an activity in Quiz. The students are going to read a paragraph and then select the correct concluding sentence. Afterwards, we are going to create an **Online text** within Assignment where they will write about the place they have just read about.

How to do it...

We are going to enter the course and select the Weekly outline section where we want to add this activity so that we can design it.

1. Click on **Add an activity** and select the **Quiz** option.
2. Complete the **Name** block with the title of the activity.
3. In the **Introduction** block, broaden the target of the activity. You can also add the link to the websites, which your students can use, to read about concluding sentences, as shown in the next screenshot:

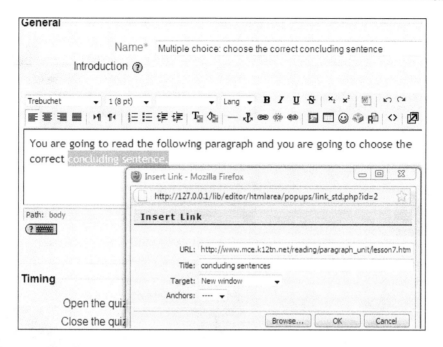

4. Complete the **Insert Link** block, as shown in the previous screenshot, and click on **OK**.

5. Click on **Save and display**.

How it works...

After saving the changes, we have to prepare the multiple choice activity. Follow these steps to finish designing the activity:

1. In **Create new question,** click on the drop-down box and click on **Multiple Choice**.

2. Complete the **Question name**.

3. Complete the **Question text**, including the paragraph that students have to read.

4. Complete the **General feedback** block with the link to the website of the Lofoten Islands, as shown in the next screenshot:

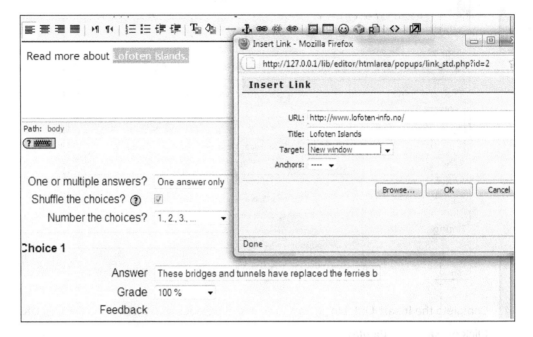

5. Click on the drop-down box in **Number the choices?** and choose the way you want to number the choices, as shown in the previous screenshot.

6. Complete **Choice 1** with the correct answer as shown in the previous screenshot.

7. In **Grade**, select **100%** as shown in the previous screenshot.

8. After writing the choices, click on **None** in **Grade**, as you are going to choose only one correct answer.

9. Complete the **Overall Feedback** blocks.

10. Click on **Save changes**.

11. Then when you click on the activity, a check appears, and then click on **Add to quiz**.

12. Click on **Save changes** and then click on **Go**.

13. Go back to the course.

There's more...

You can create an **Online text** in Assignment within add an activity so that students can write an article about the Lofoten Islands.

Mixing paragraphs

In this recipe, we are going to create a paragraph and students are going to put it in order. The easiest way to do it is through Hot Potatoes and JMix. In *Chapter 1, Connecting Ideas*, we have already done an activity using that tool, so we are not going to use it now. We are going to adapt to a game and we are going to embed it. After embedding it, use it in such a way that our students can unjumble the paragraph. I have written several times that I always add a personal touch to the methodologies and this is one of them. I propose that a paragraph be written comparing the two sagas of *Twilight* and *Harry Potter*. We are going to enter a website in which we are going to design the activity. Let's Moodle it!

Getting ready

We are going to design the activity in `http://classtools.net/`. We are going to enter this website and then select **Priority Chart**.

How to do it...

You are going to follow these steps to design the activity previously introduced:

1. Click on **Priority Chart**.
2. Complete the blocks with the paragraph mixed, as shown in the next screenshot:

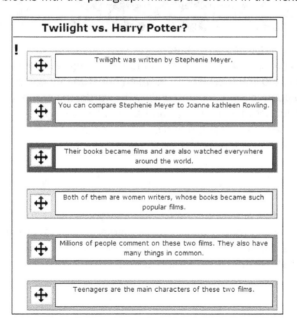

3. Click on the **Save as Web Page** icon.

How it works...

We are going to embed the activity in our Moodle course. We are going to select the Weekly outline section in which we want to insert the activity. Afterwards, we are going to follow these steps:

1. Select **Add an activity** and click on **Online text**.

2. Complete the **Assignment name** block.

3. Complete the **Description** block.

4. Go back to the website, click on the **Embed** icon, copy the Embed, and then click on **OK**.

5. Go back to the Moodle course and click on the **Toggle HTML Source** (the icon which appears like this **<>**).

6. Paste the Embed.

7. Click again on the **Toggle HTML Source** icon.

8. Click on **Save and return to course**.

9. The activity is ready to work with. Students can move the blocks and they can put them in the required order. As it is an online activity, they can write the full version and add any comments.

Selecting the correct sentences

In this recipe, we are going to work by selecting the correct sentences in a paragraph. Students will have to consider whether each sentence belongs to the paragraph or not. Therefore, we are going to link to a website in which our students can read so that they can have some idea about coherence and unity. Afterwards, the same webpage gives the opportunity to carry out activities in a cloze and students have to fill in the right connectors. Later, we are going to write a paragraph and students are going to decide if a given sentence belongs to the paragraph or not using a True/False activity in Moodle. Let's Moodle it!

Getting ready

We are going to design this activity through a Quiz in Moodle using True/False Questions. First of all, we are going to create a link to the website and then we are going to write the paragraph. Afterwards, we are going to write a paragraph and a separate sentence asking students whether it belongs to the paragraph or not.

How to do it...

We enter the course and select the Weekly outline section in which we want to add the activity. We are going to design this activity in a Quiz, so you have to follow these steps:

1. Click on **Add an activity** and select **Quiz**.

2. Complete the **Name** block with the name of the activity.

3. Complete the **Introduction** block where you are going to explain the activity and create the link to the following website: `http://lrs.ed.uiuc.edu/students/ fwalters/cohere.html`.

4. Click on **Save and display**.

How it works...

Now we will follow these steps to create an activity using True/False questions. This is an exception, but it lets us achieve our target of selecting the correct sentences! These are the steps to follow:

1. Click on the drop-down box in **Create new question**.

2. Select **True/False**.

3. Complete the **Question name** block.

4. Complete the **Question text** with the paragraph and the title, asking the students whether or not the sentences belong to the paragraph.

5. In **Correct answer**, click on the drop-down box and select **True**.

6. Complete the feedback for the response as **True** with the title of the paragraph and an explanation saying that **It is the title of the paragraph**.

7. Click on **Save changes**.

8. Click on the activity and a check will appear. Click on **Add to quiz**.

9. Click on **Go** and then click on **Save changes**.

10. The activity appears as shown in the next screenshot:

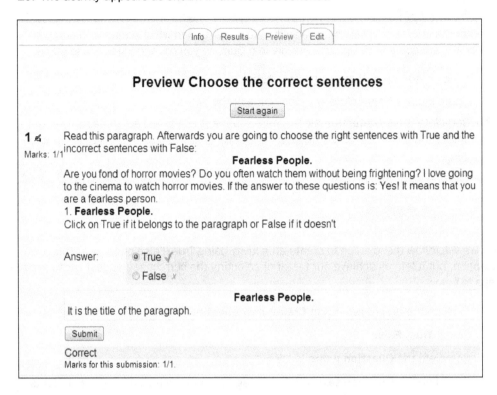

There's more...

After completing all these steps, you have just added one True/False question to the Quiz. You can write other options so that students decide whether or not these sentences fit in the paragraph.

Adding more True/False questions in the Quiz

You are going to follow these steps to add more questions so that students can choose all the correct answers in their paragraph:

1. Click on **Edit**.

2. Afterwards, you will come across the screen where we have added the True/False activities. Then follow the previous steps.

3. Write the next sentence in the paragraph in the **Question text** block, so that students check whether it belongs to the paragraph or not.

Adding detailed sentences

In this recipe, we are going to ask the students to add detailed sentences. We are going to provide students with a topic sentence and a concluding one. We are going to design this activity in Assignments and then select **Offline activity**.

Getting ready

We are going to design a very simple activity. We are going to provide our students with two types of sentences—the topic sentence and the concluding one—and they will have to complete the lines in the middle of the paragraph. They are going to add the detailed sentences. Let's Moodle it!

How to do it...

We are going to select the Weekly outline section in which we want to add the activity. Afterwards, you are going to follow these steps:

1. Click on **Add an activity** and select **Offline activity**.

2. In the **Assignment name** block, write the title of the activity.

3. Complete the **Description** block with the instructions as well as the topic and concluding sentences of the paragraph that the students have to complete.

4. Click on **Save and return to course**.

How it works...

Students are going to upload their complete paragraphs to the Moodle course. You can also add a link to a website giving more explanation about detailed sentences. You may want to include a screenshot in order to give students more ideas about the paragraph.

Writing topics and concluding sentences

In this recipe, we are going to write three topics and concluding sentences, leaving out the detailed sentences. Therefore, our students will have to write them. We are going to carry out the activity in **Advanced uploading of files**. This is done so that our students can upload three different files with the three paragraphs or they can do it in the same document. Thus, they have two options. Let's Moodle it!

Getting ready

We have to think of three different topics to write three excellent topic sentences and three concluding ones. What can we write about? How about cities? Chicago, New York, and San Francisco? Do you agree?

How to do it...

We are going to choose the Weekly outline section where we want to design the activity. So, these are the steps you have to follow:

1. Select **Add an activity** and click on the **Advanced uploading of files**.

2. Complete the **Assignment name** block with the name of the activity.

3. In the **Description** block, write what the students have to do and the three topics and concluding sentences. In this case, you can choose topics other than the cities.

4. You can also create three links to websites that give information about these cities.

5. In **Maximum number of uploaded files**, choose **3** because that is the number of files that students are to upload.

6. Click on **Save and return to course**.

How it works...

The activity is already designed for our students to work with. They can upload three different files. They may also add some pictures to the files and write some notes when they submit the files. Let's wait and see what they can write.

Hamburger paragraph: writing a composition using three types of sentences

In this recipe, I suggest that we write a paragraph using a burger diagram, which is going to give hints to students on what they should write. The delicious burger (don't look at it if you are hungry) is divided in such a way that it will give our students enough hints to write a proper paragraph and use the three types of sentences we have been working with.

Getting ready

We are going to design this activity once again through the webpage, `http://classtools.net/`, which I find quite interesting. We have already used the priority chart from that webpage in a previous recipe in this chapter. Now it is the turn of the hamburger. Let's take advantage of the resources of Web 2.0 and complete the hamburger. I have also found that this type of activity can be done with a birthday cake, so another possibility is to upload an image of a cake to the Moodle course. You are free to choose. Let's Moodle it!

How to do it...

Go to `http://classtools.net/` and follow these steps:

1. Click on **Hamburger**.

2. Complete the **Burger diagram**, as shown in the following screenshot:

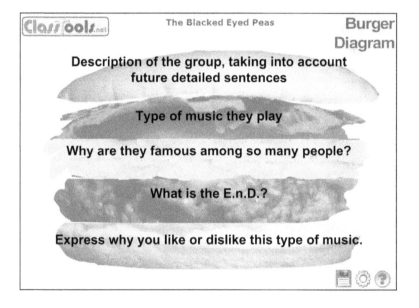

How it works...

We are going to select the Weekly outline section where we want to design this activity. This time we are going to do it through a Journal, but this activity can also be carried out in **Online text** in Assignments. You can choose an alternate option. We are also going to link to the webpage of The Black Eyed Peas where students can read their biography. You have to follow these steps:

1. Click on **Add an activity** and select **Journal**.

2. Complete the **Journal name** with the title of the activity.

3. Complete the **Journal question**.

4. Create a link to the following webpage:
   `http://blackeyedpeas.dipdive.com/biography/`.

5. Embed the hamburger to the **Journal question**.

6. Go back to the hamburger webpage and click on the icon that says **Embed into Blog/webpage**.

7. Copy the **Embed**.

8. Go back to the Moodle course.

9. Click on the **Toggle HTML Source** icon (it looks like this: **<>**).

10. Paste the **Embed**.

11. Click on the **Toggle HTML Source** icon again.

12. Click on **Save and return to course**.

13. The activity is ready to work with!

5
Creating Stories using Twitter and Facebook

In this chapter, we are going to add social networks to Moodle using Web 2.0 as a resource. We are going to incorporate Twitter and Facebook, due to the fact that these social networks are popular all over the world. We are including them in our course to incorporate the students' routines in their homework to enhance and interest their work. We have already used them in one of the recipes in *Chapter 1, Connecting Ideas*, but this chapter is going to deal exclusively with both of these networks. We are going to create different activities in them. After the activities have been created, students have to gather information in different ways and create stories. I hope that you find this chapter entertaining, as I believe that your students will!

It is very important to highlight that there exist some education privacy issues in different countries, which teachers have to be aware of before advising students to sign up for social networking. For instance, **Family Educational Rights and Privacy Act (FERPA)** protects students' rights and privacy. For more information, enter the following website: http://www2.ed.gov/policy/gen/guid/fpco/ferpa/index.html.

In this chapter, we will cover the following topics:

- Debating about a topic
- Cause and effect diagram, Fishbone fact or Ishikawa diagram: (http://en.wikipedia.org/wiki/Ishikawa_diagram)
- Positive and negative points list
- Play the reporter
- Writing a story guessing facts
- Writing a very short play using text messages
- Chain composition
- How to summarize information

Introduction

In this chapter, you will learn how to use Web 2.0 to help students interact amongst themselves in the virtual classroom using Twitter and Facebook. In addition, the students will also learn to perform difficult tasks in Moodle 1.9.5. We are going to use Twitter when we need keywords, few facts, and short statements. We are going to use Facebook to get more data, longer sentences, a short paragraph, some pictures, and so on.

You will also be able to design several types of Exercises after adding social material to the Moodle course. We are going to include two popular social networks. We are going to incorporate these networks into the Moodle course and we are also going to include different types of methodologies. This is done so that our students have several options to gather ideas for their pieces of writing. We are going to use Facebook and Twitter as resources from Web 2.0. Afterwards, we are also going to design the activities in Wikis and Forums. This allows the students to interact amongst themselves within the Moodle course.

In this virtual classroom, we are going to enrich the use of several well-known techniques using popular resources. Instead of sitting around a round table, we are going to ask our students to debate their ideas through Twitter as you will see in the first recipe. We are also going to incorporate management theories into education—for example, Fishbone fact fish or Ishikawa diagram, which is mainly used in business administration. We are going to teach it to our students so that they can create excellent pieces of writing, taking into account cause and effect.

We are going to deal with many topics, which may lead to discussion. Therefore, students can start writing argumentative essays without even realizing it. The most important detail is that we hand them the right tools to work with. In that way, they will be using keywords or phrases, which they will gather from Twitter or Facebook and they will create excellent pieces of writing. Let's Moodle it!

Debating a topic

In this task, we are going to use a methodology that we have already used many times in a debate, though it will be used virtually using resources from Web 2.0. In this recipe, we are going to use Twitter because what we need are simple statements. We are going to ask our students to debate on the following topic: what similarities or differences do they find between *The Lord of the Rings*, and *Chronicles of Narnia*. We are going to create a link to a website, which illustrates some differences and similarities. Afterwards, we are to use Twitter, and finally they are going to write their opinion in a Journal in Moodle. So, let's get started!

Getting ready

We can create an account in Twitter using the name of the subject, activity, or just our name, but let's use the account only to carry out the activities in the Moodle course. Therefore, students can follow the activities and nobody should change the course of the activity. They only have to focus on the activity.

How to do it...

Enter the Twitter webpage—http://twitter.com—create an account or use the one you have, it's your choice. If you want to create an account, click on **Sign up now** and complete the required information. Afterwards, you are going to write on what students are going to debate on as shown in the next screenshot:

1. Click on **Home.**

2. Complete the **What's happening?** block, as shown in the previous screenshot.

3. Click on **Update.**

The debate activity in Twitter is ready to work with!

How it works...

We are going to choose the Weekly outline section where we want to add the activity in the Moodle course. Afterwards, we are going to create the rest of the activity in a Journal. Follow these steps:

1. Complete the **Journal name** block: **Debating using Twitter.**

2. Complete the **Journal question** block by writing the instructions that students have to follow in order to carry out the activity, as shown in the screenshot that follows.

3. You will create a link to the Twitter account webpage, where the students are going to debate.

4. Change **Days available** to **2 weeks**, due to the fact that they are debating and it may take more than seven days, as shown in the next screenshot:

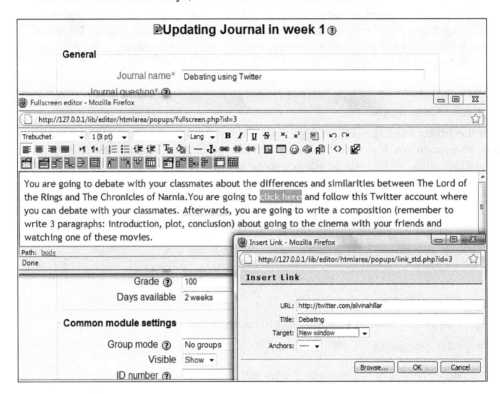

5. Later, click on **Save and return to course**.

There's more...

Instead of creating a link to the Twitter website, we can include a Twitter button in our Moodle course.

Inserting a Twitter button in Moodle

It is very simple. In order to add a Twitter button, you have to follow these steps:

1. Go to the website: `http://twitterbuttons.org/`.

2. Complete the block with your ID, as shown in the next screenshot:

3. Enter your ID and click on **GO**, as shown in the next screenshot:

4. Select the Twitter button that you like most and click on **Select Code**, as shown in the next screenshot:

5. If the chosen button is the one on the right-hand side, then right-click and select **Copy** in the context menu that appears.

6. Go to the Moodle course.

7. Update the Journal activity, and click on the **Toggle HTML Source** icon, (which looks like this: **<>**).

8. Paste that code.

9. The button will appear as shown in the next screenshot:

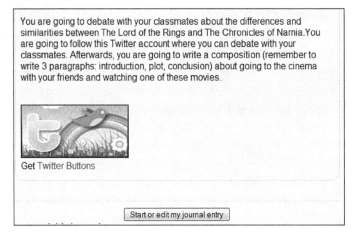

Inserting a Twitter button in the HTML block in the Moodle course

You can also insert the Twitter button in the HTML block in the Moodle course, following the previous steps instead of inserting it in the activity. The difference is that students can see the Twitter button in the Moodle course, as shown in the next screenshot:

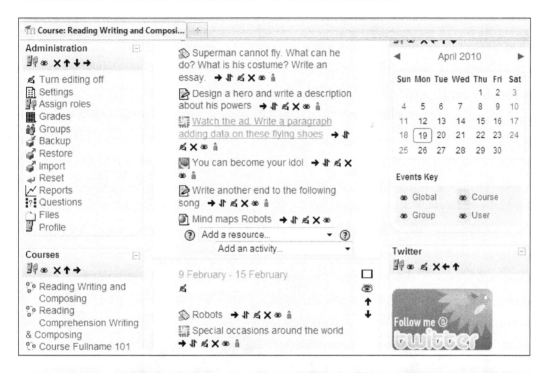

Cause-and-effect diagram, Fishbone, or Ishikawa diagram technique

In this recipe, you are going to teach your students how to design a cause and effect diagram. This diagram was created by Kaoru Ishikawa. Students can learn more about this diagram at http://en.wikipedia.org/wiki/Ishikawa_diagram. He pioneered quality management processes and he became an important person in modern management. He worked for Kawasaki shipyards. The shape of this diagram resembles the skeleton of a fish, hence the name "fishbone diagram".

This diagram explores the causes that have a single effect. There are four causes to be explored, which have details to be added. To create this diagram, you have to bear in mind some simple steps such as set a topic, identify the most important causes, and add appropriate details to them. Don't panic! It's easy. Let's Moodle it!

Getting ready

As I have already mentioned, we are going to design a fishbone diagram. We can design it using several options. You are going to select the most suitable one. There is open source and free source software to create this diagram, as well as commercial. Let's explore our choices.

How to do it...

First of all, we are going to create our fishbone diagram. The idea is that the students should complete the diagram using Facebook. Afterwards, they are going to write an essay, which is the most appropriate type of writing for this technique. The topic of the diagram is going to be the essay title; the four causes are going to be the opening topic sentences of each paragraph in the essay, and the effects are going to be the detailed sentences in each paragraph of this essay.

In this case, we are going to design an unfinished fishbone diagram using Edraw (http://www.edrawsoft.com). Then we are going to upload it to our Moodle course. So follow these steps:

1. Open Edraw and select the **Cause and Effect (Fishbone)** diagram, as shown in the next screenshot:

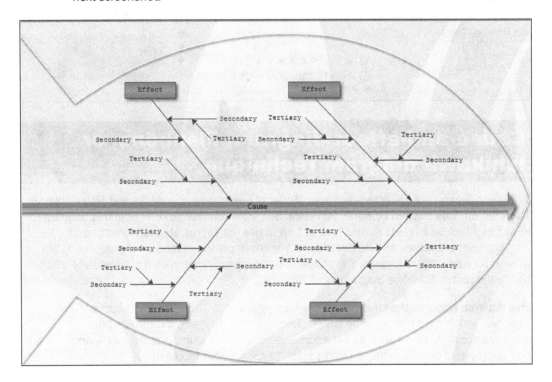

2. Click on **New** and design the fishbone diagram using the shapes on the left-hand side, as shown in the next screenshot:

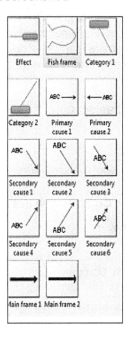

3. Draw the fishbone diagram and complete parts of it, as shown in the next screenshot:

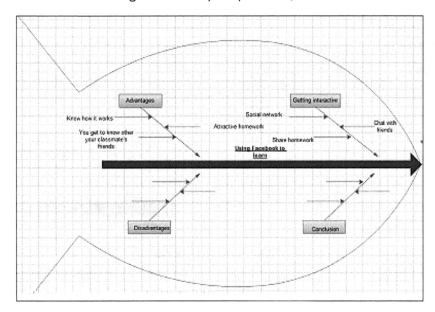

4. Click on **Save** to save this file.

How it works...

After creating the first half of the fishbone diagram, we are going to create the activity in Moodle. Before that, as we are going to use Facebook, we will either open an account for this activity or use an existing one. The website is `http://www.facebook.com`. Then we are going to enter the Weekly outline section where we want to add the activity. Later, you have to follow these steps:

1. Click on **Add an activity** and select **Quiz**.

2. Complete the **Name** block.

3. Complete the **Introduction** block.

4. Click on **Save and display**.

5. Click on the drop-down box in **Create a new question** and select **Essay**.

6. Complete the **Question name**.

7. Complete the **Question text**.

8. Click on the insert image icon. Complete it as shown in the next screenshot:

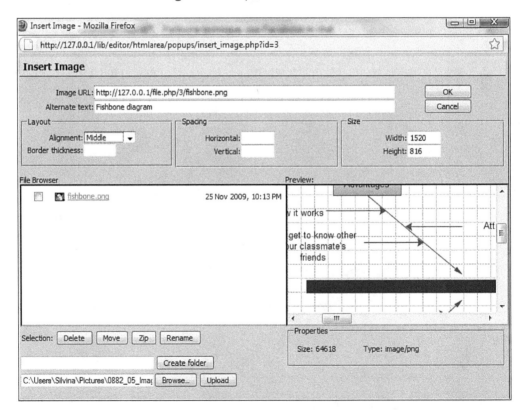

9. Click on **OK**.

10. Create a link to the Facebook web page, as shown in the next screenshot:

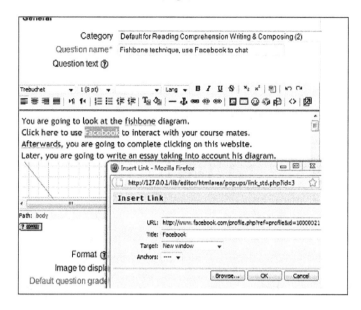

11. Complete the **Insert Link** block, as shown in the previous screenshot.

12. Then click on **OK**.

13. Afterwards, we will link to another website where students are going to complete the fishbone diagram, as shown in the next screenshot:

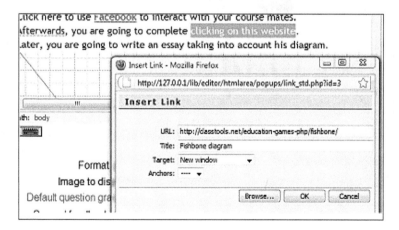

14. Complete the **Insert Link** block, as shown in the previous screenshot.

15. Then click on **OK**.

16. Click on **Save changes**.

17. Check the activity and click on **Add to quiz.**

18. Click on **Go** and then click on **Save changes**.

19. Go back to the course.

Wow! The activity is ready to work with. Try it out!

There's more...

Instead of creating a link to Facebook, we can include a Facebook button in our Moodle course.

Inserting a Facebook button in our Moodle course

It is very simple. In order to add a Facebook button, you have to follow these steps:

1. Go to the following website: `http://www.socialmediabuttons.com/facebook-buttons.html`.

2. Complete the block with your ID, as shown in the next screenshot:

3. Enter your ID and click on **GO**.

4. Select the Facebook button that you like most and click on **Select Code**, as shown in the following screenshot:

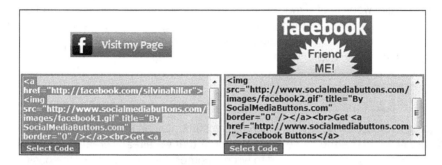

5. If the select button is the one on the left-hand side, then right-click and select **Copy** in the context menu that appears.

6. Go to the Moodle course.

7. Update the **Essay** and click on the **Toggle HTML Source** icon (which looks like this: **<>**).

8. Paste the code.

9. The button will appear as shown in the following screenshot:

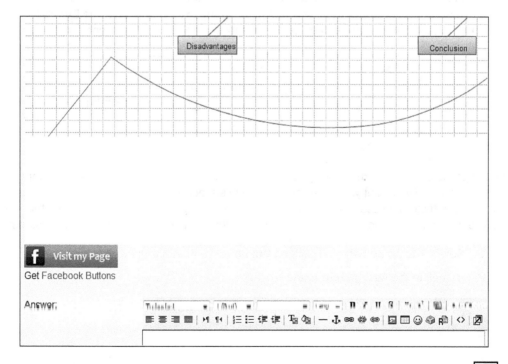

Positive and negative points list

In this recipe, we are going to create a positive and negative points list. We are going to create a link to the official website of Alnwick Castle, which is in England. This castle can be rented for a wedding or a special celebration with friends. Through Twitter, students can give either positive or negative feedback about renting the castle for their graduation party. Wouldn't that be awesome? Let's Moodle it!

Getting ready

We are going to create an activity in which all the students can give their opinion about this idea. We are going to use the same Twitter account that we already created for the previous activity. Afterwards, students are going to write a composition using either the positive list or the negative one. They are going to use only one list because they are going to write a story depending on what happened in their graduation party. This story can either be positive or negative. Another option is to write an essay about the advantages and disadvantages of planning a graduation party in a castle. I'm going to propose the first one so that they learn how to write stories using different techniques.

How to do it...

Let's propose the activity to our students in Twitter. Therefore we are going to enter the Twitter account we have previously created. We are going to add the title of the Exercise by completing the **What's happening?** block, as shown in the next screenshot:

What's happening?	2
Positive and negative points list: Let's do a gratudation party in Alnwick Castle. Check: http://www.alnwickcastle.com/weddings-venue-hire	

How it works...

We are going to enter into the Weekly outline section in our Moodle course where we want to add the activity. If you want your students to write in support of or against an article, you can design the activity in an Essay. But, if you want your students to invent a story using either the positive or the negative points, then you can use **Online text**. You have to follow these steps:

1. Select **Add an activity** and click on **Online text** within Assignments.

2. Complete the **Assignment name** block.

3. Complete the **Description** block. In this block, link to Twitter, as shown in the next screenshot:

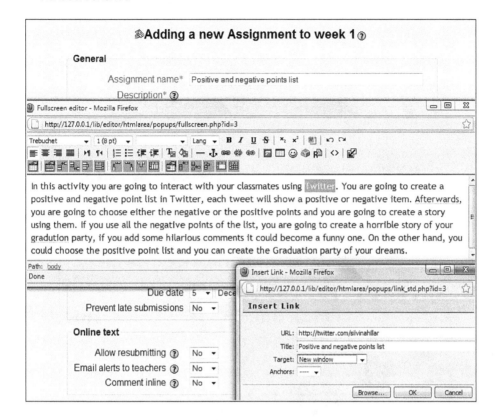

4. Complete the **Insert Link** block, as shown in the previous screenshot.

5. Click on **Save and return to course**.

The activity is ready to work with.

There's more...

Instead of creating a link to Twitter website, we can include a Twitter button in our Moodle course.

Inserting a Twitter button in Moodle

It is very simple. In order to add a Twitter button, you have to follow these steps:

1. Go to the following website: `http://twitterbuttons.sociableblog.com/`. You have to follow the instructions given on the web page.

2. Complete the block with your ID, as shown in the next screenshot:

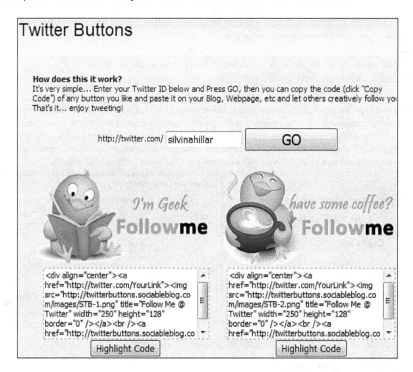

3. Enter your ID and click on **GO**, as shown in the previous screenshot.

4. Choose the Twitter button that you like best and click on **Highlight Code**.

5. Right-click and select **Copy** in the context menu that appears.

6. Go to the Moodle course.

7. Update the Assignment and click on the **Toggle HTML Source** icon, (which looks like this: **<>**).

8. Paste this code.

9. The icon will appear as shown in the next screenshot:

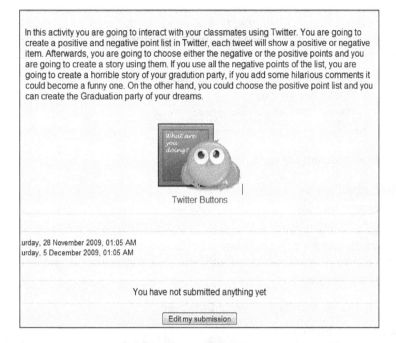

In this activity you are going to interact with your classmates using Twitter. You are going to create a positive and negative point list in Twitter, each tweet will show a positive or negative item. Afterwards, you are going to choose either the negative or the positive points and you are going to create a story using them. If you use all the negative points of the list, you are going to create a horrible story of your gradution party, if you add some hilarious comments it could become a funny one. On the other hand, you could choose the positive point list and you can create the Graduation party of your dreams.

What are you doing?

Twitter Buttons

urday, 28 November 2009, 01:05 AM
urday, 5 December 2009, 01:05 AM

You have not submitted anything yet

Edit my submission

Play the reporter

In this recipe, we will be designing three different activities in order to help our students to write a story. First of all, they are to use Twitter to interact amongst themselves about a crime (either a felony or a misdemeanor) that has occurred lately. Then, we are going to create a Database in Moodle so that they can answer the five "wh" questions. The last activity is the piece of writing that they'll have to carry out while uploading a file.

Getting ready

We are going to create a discussion in Twitter about a crime that has occurred lately. It would be great to have the latest piece of news. So, I am going to design the activity with the latest news in my neighborhood that: 'The Brown family is missing'. A complete family has been missing for more than 20 days. Nobody knows where they are. Shall we design the activity? Let's Moodle it!

How to do it...

You are going to enter Twitter (remember that you can use the account for the Moodle course), and you are going to complete the **What's happening?** block, as shown in the next screenshot:

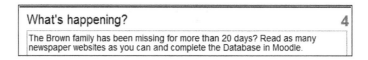

What's happening?   4

The Brown family has been missing for more than 20 days? Read as many
newspaper websites as you can and complete the Database in Moodle.

Click on **Update** and the activity is introduced in Twitter.

How it works...

You are going to enter the Weekly outline section where you want to insert the activity in Moodle. Afterwards, you are going to create a Database. We have to bear in mind that Database cannot be marked or assessed with information stored in the grade book. You have to follow these steps:

1. Click on **Add an activity** and select **Database**.

2. Complete the **Name** block.

3. Complete the **Introduction** block. You are going to link to the Twitter website, as shown in the next screenshot:

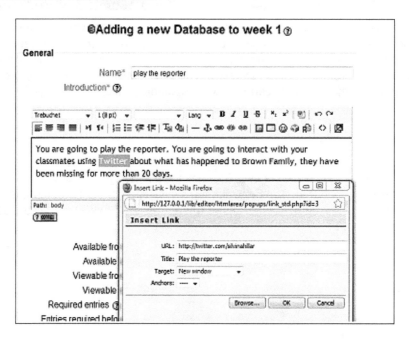

4. Complete the **Insert Link** block as shown in the previous screenshot.

5. Click on **Save and display.**

6. In **Create a new field,** click on the drop-down box and select **Text.**

7. You are going to complete the **Field name** block with a question, as shown in the next screenshot:

8. Click on **Add.**

9. Repeat the process five times. The final result is shown in the next screenshot:

10. Click on **Save**.

11. Go back to the course. The activity is ready to work with.

There's more...

This is where the writing activity is going to be designed. In earlier chapters, we guided the writing of our students using questions. However, in this case, we have done something similar in a different and interactive way.

Creating a writing activity using the answers in the Database

Students have discussed amongst themselves about a crime. After the discussion, they have answered the questions about what they think might have happened. Now, it is time for them to write the story. Let's carry out the activity by following these steps:

1. Click on **Add an activity** and select **Upload a single file** within Assignments.

2. Complete the **Assignment name** block.

3. Complete the **Description** block, as shown in the next screenshot:

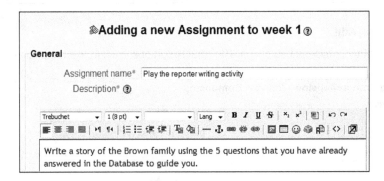

4. Click on **Save and return to course**.

Tweeting in an easier way

You can show your students how to install TweetDeck. It is a free and popular application, which allows tweeting in an easier way. You can download this application from `http://www.tweetdeck.com/`, as shown in the next screenshot:

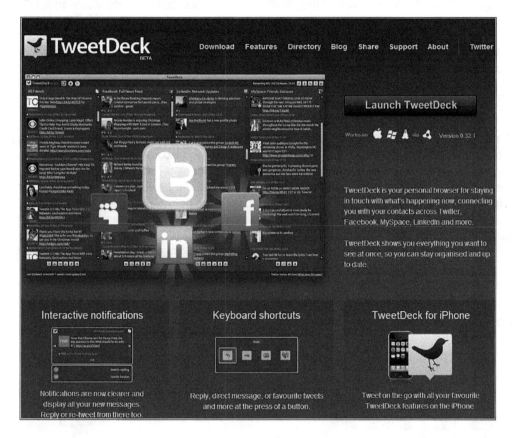

You have to click on **Download** and follow the steps. You can tweet as shown in the background of the previous screenshot. Tiny automatic URLs are also available in this application. You can also use it in your iPhone, iPad, or iPod. Another great advantage is that when you click on a picture, you can tweet again, reply, or send a direct message to a person easily. This can be done by clicking on the desired option in **Keyboard shortcuts** as shown in the previous screenshot.

Writing a story guessing facts

In this recipe, we are going to take advantage of the public albums in Facebook! We are going to ask our students to select one of their contacts from this social network. Afterwards, the students will go through the photo album that they have created and write a story based on it. They may also include the pictures that belong to their friends who already know the real story. In this case, we are not going to guide our students in order to write a story, but we will provide hints on how to be creative enough so as to write a good one.

Getting ready

We are going to design this activity in Facebook and in Moodle. I have selected Facebook, as the photo album is included in it. In addition, comments are also added to the pictures. These comments provide hints on the story to be written. One writing technique, which is useful in case you are out of ideas, is to refer to a book or a newspaper. Select one word and you can think of something related to this word. You can use this to add to your story. In the same way, our students can take ideas from the comments added to the pictures if they run out their own.

How to do it...

You are going to enter the Facebook website and you are going to complete the **Live Feed** block, as shown in the following screenshot:

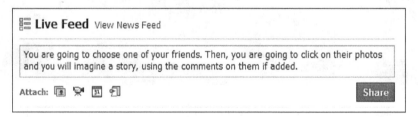

Then, you are going to click on **Share**. The activity is ready in Facebook. Let's Moodle it!

How it works...

We are going to design the activity in Wiki so that if the students are in the photos, they can write a collective story. So, you are going to enter the Weekly outline section where you want to add the activity. You are going to follow these steps:

1. Click on **Add an activity** and select **Wiki**.
2. Complete the **Name** block.
3. Complete the **Summary** block and link to the Facebook website.
4. Click on **Save and return to course**.

The activity is ready for your students to work with.

Writing a very short play using text messages

We are going to carry out this activity through Facebook. We are going to create a group where students can interact amongst themselves and upload some pictures. Later, with all the information that they have obtained, they are going to write a play. We are going to design the activity in Moodle in **Advanced uploading of files**. The idea is that they create different types of writing. That is the reason why a play is also included in the recipes. Let's get ready!

Getting ready

We are going to enter the Facebook website and we are going to create a group. We are going to design a group activity so as to encourage our students to work with it. We are also going to impose some restrictions on the group. We are not going to make this group activity a public one but just for the members of our Moodle course.

How to do it...

Before creating the activity in Moodle, we have to create the activity group in Facebook. So, we are going to enter Facebook and follow these steps:

1. Click on the **Group** icon, the one with two persons, as shown in the next screenshot:

2. Click on **Create a New Group**.

3. You are going to complete **Step1: Group Info**, as shown in the next screenshot:

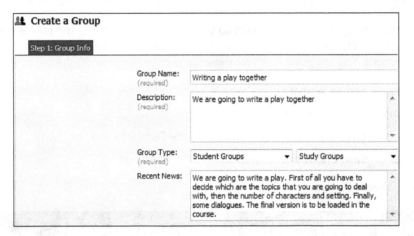

4. After completing all the information, click on **Create Group**.

5. Complete **Step 2: Customize**, as shown in the next screenshot:

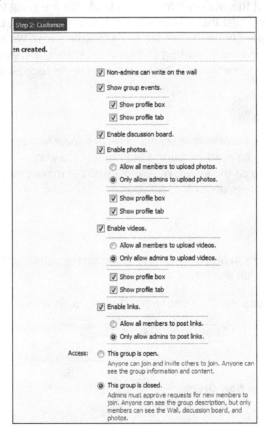

6. Click on **Save**.

7. Invite your students to join the group that has just been created. They can only interact if you invite them because this group is closed, as shown in the previous screenshot.

How it works...

Select the Weekly outline section where you want to carry out the activity in the Moodle course. You are going to design this activity in **Advanced uploading of files**. It is a good option to carry out this kind of activity because students can write the play offline and then upload it to the Moodle course. Follow these steps:

1. Click on **Add an activity** and select **Advanced uploading of files** within Assignments.

2. Complete the **Assignment name** block.

3. Complete the **Description** block and create a link to the Facebook website as shown in the next screenshot:

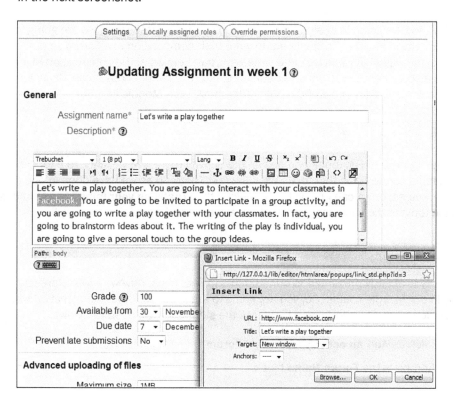

4. Complete the **Insert Link** block, as shown in the previous screenshot, and click on **OK**.

5. Click on **Save and return to course**.

The activity is ready for your students to write!

Chain composition

In this recipe, I have adapted chain writing. In the old fashioned way, students were given a topic, a piece of paper, and a pen. They had to write a sentence and after a period of time (say, one to three minutes), they had to pass the paper to their classmates so that they could finish the composition. Now we are going to update this technique using Facebook as the piece of paper and the keyboard as the pen. We are also going to add a special ingredient to this recipe—the time will be one week. Let's get ready to work!

Getting ready

First of all, we are going to design the activity in Facebook. Afterwards, we are going to carry out the activity in Moodle. Students are to write their composition in a Forum so that everyone can use all the ideas in Facebook and write their own version of the composition in a Forum. They can also gather ideas from other students, but they cannot copy those ideas. We will know who wrote first because of the date of the post. Let's Moodle it!

How to do it...

We are going to go to Facebook and design the activity there. We will choose a topic so that students can write on that topic. We can create a group as we have done in one of the previous recipes, or we can just write the topic in the **What's on your mind?** block. In this case, the topic of the composition is My house is a plane.

How it works...

The activity is already presented to our students in Facebook, now we have to present the activity in our Moodle course. So, you are going to enter the Weekly outline section where you want to design the activity and these are the steps that you need to follow:

1. Click on **Add an activity** and select **Forum**.

2. Complete the **Forum Name** block.

3. Complete the **Forum introduction** block.

4. Create a link to the Facebook website where students can interact with their classmates and gather the data for the composition, as shown in the next screenshot:

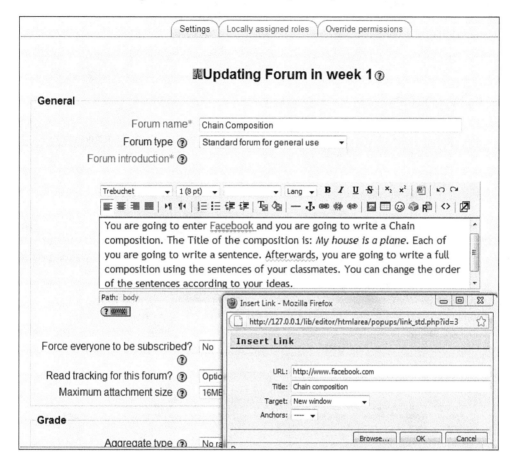

5. Complete the **Insert Link** block, as shown in the previous screenshot, and click on **OK**.

6. Click on **Save and return to course**.

Students can work with this activity, and they can also upload a file with their writing.

How to summarize information

In this recipe, I suggest that we keep the writing short and simple. This is the reason that we are going to use Twitter. We are going to ask our students to write about how they feel during a certain period of the year—for example, we may choose the end of the year, a national holiday, or a special event in their lives. After students tweet about a certain topic, they are going to complete a Journal and complete a small piece of writing.

Getting ready

We are going to enter the Twitter web page and design the first part of the activity there. It is going to be very simple. We will select a topic attractive to teenagers.

How to do it...

Enter Twitter (remember that you can use the account for the Moodle course) and complete the **What's happening?** block after selecting the topic that we are going to tweet to our students. In this case, we are going to deal with the topic of how they will be spending their next holidays.

Now enter `http://tinyurl.com/` where we can shorten the URL due to text length limitations in Twitter, as shown in the next screenshot. So, we can choose a destination for the students' holiday, search for a website, copy the URL, and paste it in **Enter a long URL to make tiny**. Click on **Make Tiny URL!**. Afterwards, you paste that tiny URL in Twitter.

Welcome to TinyURL!™

Are you sick of posting URLs in emails only to have it break when sent causing the recipient to have to cut and paste it in a URL in the text field below, we will create a tiny URL that *will not break in email postings* and *never expires*.

Enter a long URL to make tiny:

[   ] [Make TinyURL!]

Custom alias (optional):

http://tinyurl.com/ [   ]

May contain letters, numbers, and dashes.

An example

Turn this URL:

http://rover.ebay.com/rover/1/711-53200-19255-0/1?t
ype=3&campid=5336224516&toolid=10001&customid=tiny-
hp&ext=unicycle&satitle=unicycle

into this tinyURL:

http://tinyurl.com/unicycles

Which one would you rather cut and paste into your browser? That's the power of TinyURL!

Add TinyURL to your browser's toolbar

To track all the tweets related to a certain topic use # tags—for example, # vacations. In this case, you are going to have all the tweets that contain the word vacation, that is to say when you add the tweet and click on this word, you have all the tweets related to this topic.

How it works...

We are going to select the Weekly outline section where we want to add the activity in the Moodle course. Afterwards, we are going to create the rest of the activity in a Journal, (you can also carry out the activity in **Online text** within Assignments). Follow these steps:

1. Complete the **Journal name** block.

2. Complete the **Journal question** block.

3. You are going to create a link to the Twitter account web page.

4. Later, click on **Save and return to course**.

6
Improving Your Students' Writing

In this chapter, we are going to improve the writing of our students through the **cubing technique**. We are going to use a prewriting technique. This technique explores six different perspectives. First, you have to select a topic, person, problem, among others to explore. Students are to explore the same topic from six different perspectives as the sides of a cube. We are going to incorporate the cube in the Moodle course. In each recipe, we are going to deal with a different topic and we are going to explore a different side or perspective and the cube will show that aspect.

We are going to list the six perspectives of the cubing technique. Next to each perspective, we are going to have some keywords or questions so as to develop the aspects extensively. These are the perspectives with a brief description for each of them:

- ▶ Describe—description of the topic and identification of its parts
- ▶ Compare—similarities and differences of one topic to other topics
- ▶ Associate—relationship between the current topic and another one. Compare it to another topic it makes you think of
- ▶ Analyze—relationship between the components of the topic and its parts
- ▶ Apply—usage of the topic
- ▶ Argue—arguments for and against the topic

In the last activity, we are going to incorporate a **rolling cube** and also cover how to correct an essay. Therefore, students will be attracted to the proposed Assignments, because they are quite appealing.

Introduction

In this chapter, you will be able to design seven activities involving the use of the cubing technique. The first six activities will only involve the use of one aspect of the cube. In the seventh recipe, we are going to include a rolling cube. So the students have to perform the cubing technique based on one topic. This technique is quite interesting, and apart from that we are going to insert a cube in each of the recipes in our Moodle course.

In this virtual classroom, we are going to enrich the use of prewriting methodologies. That is the reason we are going to develop this step by step. Students will deal with each side of the cube individually. Let's Moodle it!

Cubing technique: Describe

In this task, we are going to deal with the description of a topic. We are going to match this angle of the cube with the order of adjectives that has to be followed when describing something. We can either create a link to a website, which gives information about this topic, or we can upload an explanation from Microsoft PowerPoint.

Getting ready

Let's create a passive activity in Microsoft PowerPoint. We are going to create a receptive activity in which students are going to read about the normal order of adjectives:

1. Opinion.
2. Size.
3. Quality.
4. Age.
5. Shape.
6. Color.
7. Origin.
8. Material.
9. Purpose.

Students should bear in mind that we normally don't use more than three adjectives before a noun. So let's create a document in Microsoft PowerPoint. You can also use OpenOffice to create a document so that we can upload it into our Moodle course afterwards.

How to do it...

After creating the document in Microsoft PowerPoint, we are going to upload it into Moodle. Enter the course and select the Weekly outline section where you want to add the resource. Then follow these steps:

1. Click on the drop-down box in **Add a resource** and select **Link to a file or website**.

2. Complete the **Name** block.

3. Complete the **Summary** block.

4. Click on **Choose or upload a file**.

5. Click on **Upload a file**.

6. Click on **Browse** and select the file that you want to upload.

7. Click on **Upload this file**.

8. Check the file that you want to upload and click on **Choose**, as shown in the next screenshot:

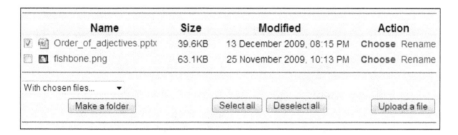

9. In **Target**, select **New window**.

10. Afterwards, you have to click on **Save and return to course**.

How it works...

After uploading the Microsoft PowerPoint presentation in Moodle, we are going to design the activity concerning the cubing technique. In this recipe, we are going to deal with Dracula. As the angle of this cube will cover description, students are to describe him. We are going to upload two pictures, one picture will be the cube that says **Describe**, and the other will be a picture of Dracula so that students can describe him properly.

We are going to create a document in Microsoft Word, or any other word processor. We are going to upload an image of Dracula and a 3D cube on which we are going to write the word **Describe**, which is the perspective that students are going to work with. Afterwards, we are going to copy and paste both images in Paint or any other similar software. We are going to save the images as .png and .jpeg files so that we can upload those images together in Moodle.

We are going to carry out the activity in a Forum so that students can share the different descriptions of Dracula. Follow these steps:

1. Click on **Add an activity** and select **Forum**.

2. Complete **Forum name**.

3. Complete **Forum introduction**.

4. Click on the insert image icon so that we can insert the images.

5. Click on **Browse** and select the file that you have created.

6. Then click on **Open**.

7. Click on **Upload**.

8. Click on **OK**.

9. The image is uploaded, as shown in the next screenshot:

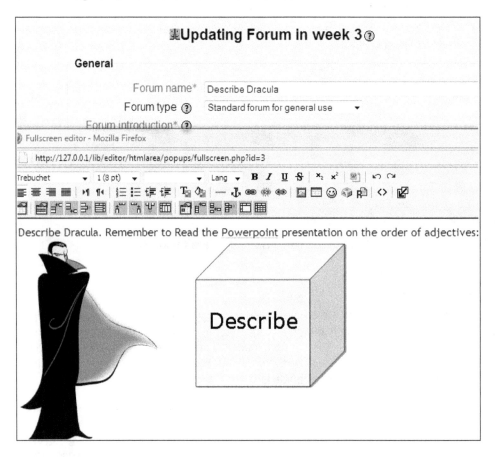

10. Click on **Save and return to course**.

There's more...

When we created both activities, either the passive or the active one, we wrote the same words. Therefore, we can link them together automatically, though this option is disabled by default. If it doesn't work, you should contact your Moodle admin to have it enabled.

Connecting both activities automatically

When we create a link to a file, we name the link as "order of adjectives". When we described the Forum in the Forum introduction, we wrote the words "order of adjectives" in the same way as we wrote the name of the file. Therefore, when students click on the Forum activity to perform it, the words **order of adjectives** will be highlighted in gray, as shown in the next screenshot:

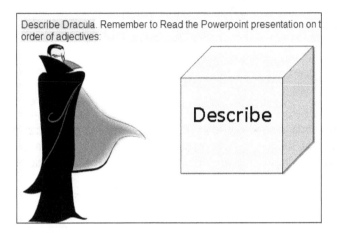

If you click on them, there is an automatic link that links to the file of the said name. The following will appear, as shown in the next screenshot:

You are going to view a Microsoft Powerpoint presentation about the order of adjectives and examples of each of them.

This resource should appear in a popup window.
If it didn't, click here: order of adjectives

Cubing technique: Compare

In this recipe, you will be designing a comparison activity. This is due to the fact that another side of the cubing technique has to do with comparisons. This technique is used with the same topic, though in this chapter we are covering a topic different from the one covered in the first recipe. This is done to give you more material to work with. In this recipe, we are dealing with "Travelling". We are going to explore the comparison, so we are going to compare travelling by cruise and travelling by plane. Let's Moodle it!

Getting ready

First of all, we should choose where we will be travelling from. This destination can be where we live or our students' live. Your students are going to imagine that they are sailing! Therefore, they are going to write a paragraph comparing travelling on a cruise to travelling by plane.

How to do it...

We are going to carry out this activity in Edraw Max. We are going to design a drawing of a world map with two options of comparison. In this case, we are going to travel from the south of England to the north of Spain. We will imagine that planes and cruises get to both destinations. So let's prepare the drawing so that we can upload it to our Moodle course afterwards.

We are also going to include a cube with the word **Compare** in it, as shown in the next screenshot:

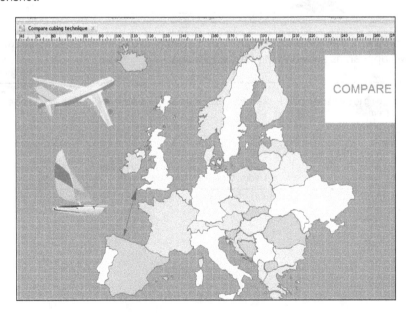

How it works...

After creating the drawing in Edraw Max in this case, you may also use a similar software. We will upload the drawing in our Moodle course so as to design the activity. Before entering the Moodle course, we are going to copy and paste the drawing into Paint or any similar software to save it as a `.png` or `.jpeg` file.

Afterwards, we are going to do the activity through a Journal. So enter the course and choose the Weekly outline section where you want to add the activity and follow these steps.

1. Click on **Add an activity** and select **Journal**.

2. Complete the **Journal name** block.

3. Complete the **Journal question** block.

4. Click on the icon to insert a picture.

5. Click on **Browse** and search for the file.

6. When you find the file, click on **Upload**.

7. Complete the **Alternate text** block, as shown in the next screenshot:

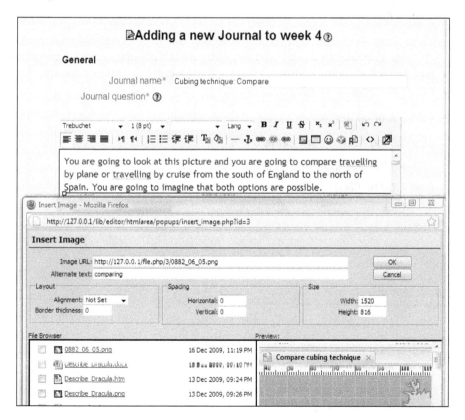

8. Click on **OK.**

9. Click on **Save and return to course**.

The activity is ready to work with!

Cubing technique: Associate

In this recipe, we are going to deal with another side of the cube as well as another topic. We are dealing with "Literature and Revenge" and we are going to associate three English classic novels. So let's get ready and Moodle it!

Getting ready

Associate has to do with the relationship between the topic and another items with similar characteristics—in other words, how the topic is composed and where it belongs. Therefore, in this recipe we are going to deal with three books: *The Man in the Iron Mask* and *The Count of Monte Cristo* by Alexander Dumas and *The Phantom of the Opera* by Gaston Leroux.

How to do it...

We are going to enter the course and select the Weekly outline section where we want to add this activity so that we can design it. In this case, we are going to carry out the activity in **Online text** and we are going to insert a table with only one row and one column so as to simulate our cube. Follow these steps:

1. Click on **Add an activity** and select **Online text** option.

2. Complete the **Assignment name** block.

3. Complete the **Description** block.

4. Insert a **Table**. Click on the table icon to insert a table.

5. Complete the **Rows** and **Cols** blocks with number **1**, as shown in the next screenshot:

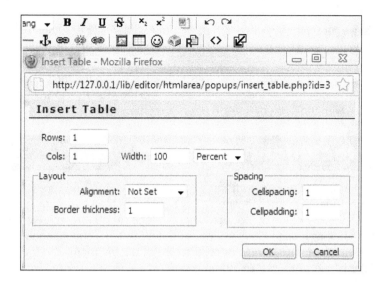

6. Click on **OK**.

7. Write the word **ASSOCIATE** in the table, as shown in the next screenshot:

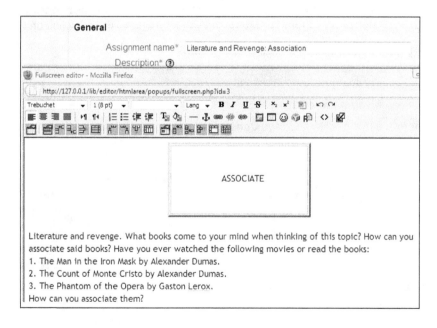

8. Complete the other blocks the way you want to.

9. Click on **Save and return to course**.

How it works...

The activity that we have just designed is ready for our students to edit their submission. In this case, we have provided the students with the name of items that they have to associate with the topic. You do not need to do that. You can always guide the writing of your students the way you want to according to the guidelines that you set. In each recipe, I think it is helpful to guide them with each angle of the cube. This will help the students to work alone and without difficulties with the cube by itself in the last recipe.

Cubing technique: Analyse

In this recipe, we are going to work with `http://www.floorplanner.com/`. We are going to propose to our students to analyze where they shall place their bedroom in the design that they are going to see. The name of the topic will be "Place your Bedroom". We are going to design a house. You may design it the way you want to. Students should analyze the natural light to take advantage of natural resources, the view of the bedroom, and the view of the other parts of the house. Let's design the house!

Getting ready

We are going to enter the following website, `http://www.floorplanner.com`. Click on **Free Signup>**. Complete your **E-mail address** and write a **Password**. Then click on **Sign up**.

After signing up, create a floor map. Follow these steps:

1. Click on **My dashboard**.
2. Click on **My first project**.
3. There are two blocks: one says **Construction** the other one says **Library**, as shown in the next screenshot:

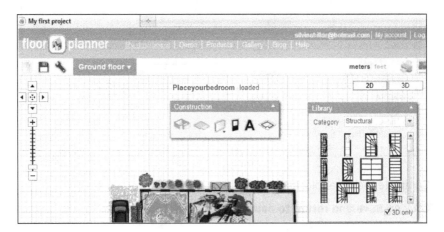

4. Click on the **Construction** icons and you can start constructing the house.

5. Click on the drop-down box in the Library Category and select what you want to insert in the plan.

6. Start designing the house that we are going to include in our Moodle course.

How to do it...

After designing the floor plan, you have to save it so that you can use it afterwards. We can create a link to the website or we can embed it into our Moodle course. Another option is to use Snipping Tool to capture the image, and copy and paste it in a Microsoft Word document where we are going to write the description of the activity to students.

You can use other applications to take screenshots instead of Snipping Tool. I have chosen this one because it is a very simple and useful application to take screenshots of rectangular areas. It is available in most modern Windows versions: Windows 7, Windows Vista, and Windows XP Tablet PC.

After taking a screenshot of the floor plan, we can upload it in our Moodle course. We are going to upload a file because we are designing the activity in an Exercise. Follow these steps to capture the image with Snipping Tool:

1. Start Snipping Tool (you can find it when you click on **Start Menu** | **All Programs** | **Accesories** | **Snipping Tool**).

2. Click on the **New** button where you can see a pair of scissors. (The screen will change its brightness and the pointer of the mouse will be a cross.)

3. Locate the mouse pointer to capture the image of the floor plan. You can also change the view of the floor plan by clicking on the **3D** icon. You can capture both images of the plan.

4. When selecting the whole floor plan, do not release the mouse button.

5. After releasing the mouse button, the image will appear in Snipping Tool software.

6. Click on **Edit** and select **Copy**.

7. Afterwards, paste the image in a Microsoft Word document in which we are going to write the activity for our students.

We are going to create the following document so that we can upload it into Exercise, as shown in the next screenshot:

How it works...

Select the Weekly outline section where you want to add the activity. In this case, we are going to carry out this activity in an Exercise, so you have to follow these steps:

1. Click on **Add an activity** and select **Exercise**.

2. Complete the **Title** block.

3. Complete the other options as you want to.

4. Click on **Save and display**.

5. Complete the **Editing Assessment Elements** blocks according to what you want to focus on, as shown in the the the next screenshot:

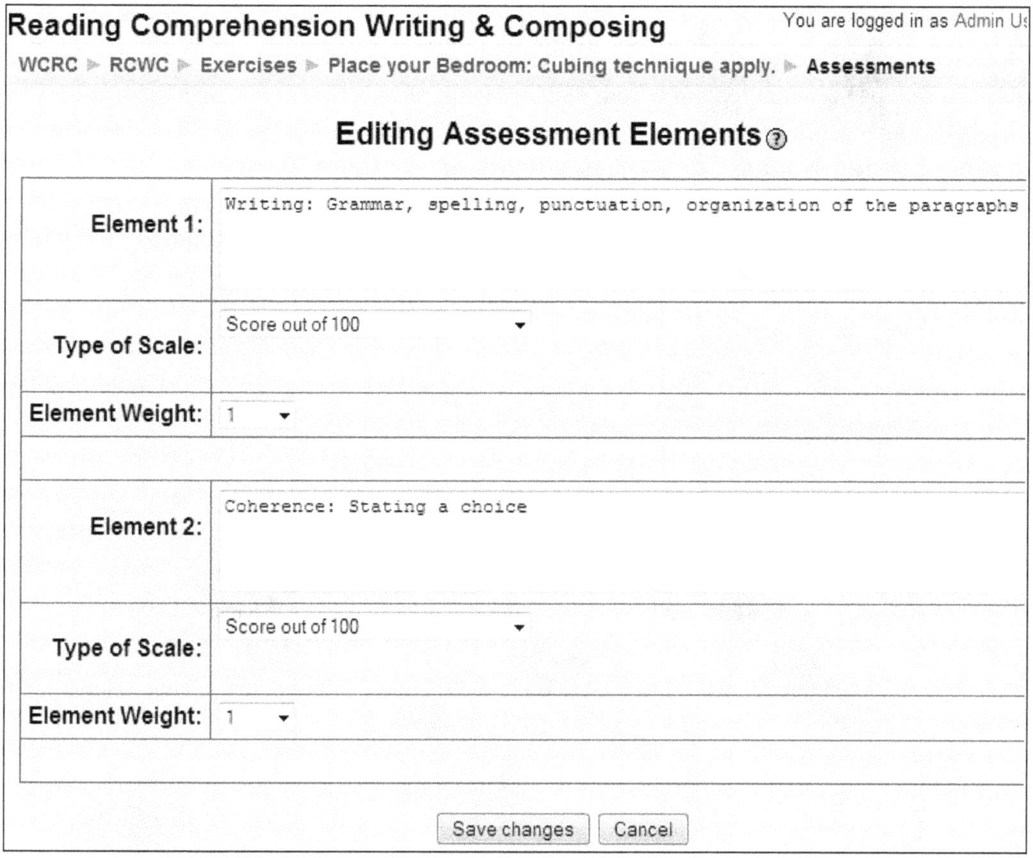

Reading Comprehension Writing & Composing   You are logged in as Admin Us

WCRC ▶ RCWC ▶ Exercises ▶ Place your Bedroom: Cubing technique apply. ▶ **Assessments**

Editing Assessment Elements ⑦

Element 1:	Writing: Grammar, spelling, punctuation, organization of the paragraphs
Type of Scale:	Score out of 100 ▾
Element Weight:	1 ▾
Element 2:	Coherence: Stating a choice
Type of Scale:	Score out of 100 ▾
Element Weight:	1 ▾

[Save changes]   [Cancel]

6. Click on **Save changes**.
7. Click on **Continue**.
8. Click on **Submit Exercise description**.
9. Click on **Browse** and look for the file containing the activity description.
10. Complete the **Title** block.
11. Click on **Upload a file**.
12. Click on **Continue**.

The activity is ready to work with!

There's more...

You can also use another resource from Web 2.0 in order to carry out this activity.

Using Sweet Home 3D to design the floor plan

We can also carry out the design of the floor plan for the house using Sweet Home 3D. It is a free interior design application. While you design the house, you can see both 2D and 3D previews. In order to launch the application, follow these steps:

1. Go to `www.sweethome3d.eu`.

2. Click on **Download**, as shown in the next screenshot:

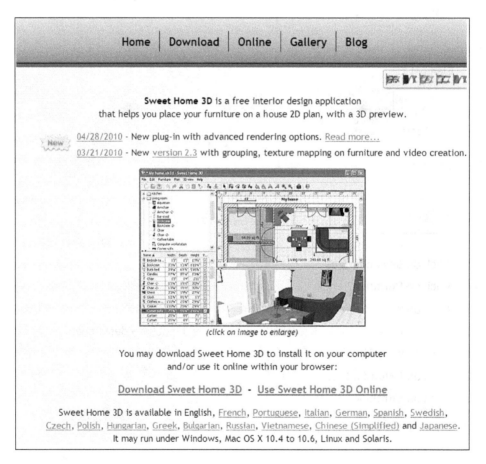

3. Click on **Launch Sweet Home 3D with Java Web Start**.

4. Click on **Run**.

5. You can design the floor plan as shown in the previous screenshot. On the left-hand side, you drag the desired element into the drawing area, and while you draw, you can see this element in 3D at the bottom of the window.

Cubing technique: Apply

In this recipe, we are going to deal with another angle of the cubing technique that is Apply. We are going to deal with the topic: "Getting lost". What do students do when they get lost? I think it is a nice topic to develop this angle of the cube particularly because Apply involves usage of the topic. We can add different elements to the situation in order to guide their thinking process.

Getting ready

We are going to design this writing activity through an Essay within the Quiz. First of all, we are going to think what elements we are to include in the situation that we are going to present our students with. After thinking about that (you are free to modify my version), we enter the course and select the Weekly outline section in which we want to add the activity. Let's Moodle it!

How to do it...

As you are going to design this activity in an Essay within a Quiz, you have to follow these steps:

1. Click on **Add an activity** and select **Quiz**.
2. Complete the **Name** block.
3. Compete the **Introduction** block.
4. Complete the other choices as you want to.
5. Click on **Save and display**.

How it works...

After completing the first part of the Quiz, we are shown another screen where we have to select the type of quiz that we want to carry out. Therefore, these are the steps to follow in order to design the activity:

1. Click on the drop-down box in **Create a new question** and select **Essay**.
2. Complete the **Question name**.

3. Complete the **Question text**, as shown in the next screenshot:

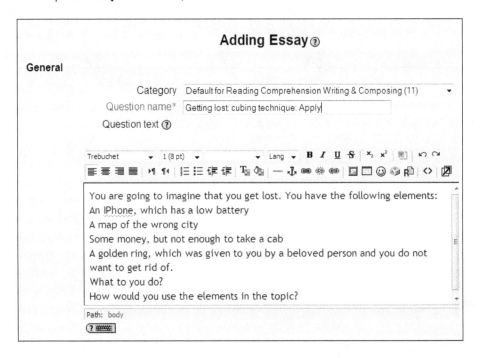

Within the screenshot:

Adding Essay ⑦

General

Category   Default for Reading Comprehension Writing & Composing (11) ▾

Question name*   Getting lost cubing technique: Apply

Question text ⑦

> You are going to imagine that you get lost. You have the following elements:
> An IPhone, which has a low battery
> A map of the wrong city
> Some money, but not enough to take a cab
> A golden ring, which was given to you by a beloved person and you do not want to get rid of.
> What to you do?
> How would you use the elements in the topic?

Path: body

4. Click on **Save changes**.

5. Check the activity that you have just created and click on **Add to quiz**.

6. Click on **Go** and then click on **Save changes**.

7. Then go back to the course.

Your students can now attempt the quiz!

Cubing technique: Argue

In this recipe, we are going to work with the last perspective of the cube, if fate allows you to roll the cube in this way! It may be one of the easiest perspectives to work with because students have to go over the for-and-against side of a topic. In this case, we are going to deal with "Taking a year off before going to college". You may or may not have have taken a year off, but your students may think about that when they finish school. So let's give them this opportunity to express their arguments.

Getting ready

We are going to combine two Moodle activities in this case. This is done to take a record of how many students in our virtual classroom would like to take a year off and how many of them would like to go on studying immediately after school (that was my case, by the way). We are going to work with **Choice** to create this "survey", and later they are going to perform their writing activity through a Lesson. So let's Moodle it!

How to do it...

Choose the Weekly outline section where you want to add the activity and then follow these steps to create a choice:

1. Click on **Add an activity** and select **Choice**.
2. Complete the **Choice name** block.
3. Complete the **Choice text** block.
4. Fill the **Choice 1** and **Choice 2** blocks, as shown in the next screenshot:

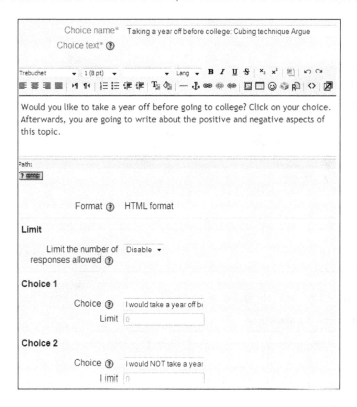

5. Click on **Save and return to course**.

How it works...

After creating the choice, we are going to design the writing activity through a Lesson. In this case, we have the possibility to upload a file in order to describe the activity. That is the reason we are going to design it in a Microsoft Word file first so as to upload it in our Moodle course afterwards. The activity is displayed in the following screenshot:

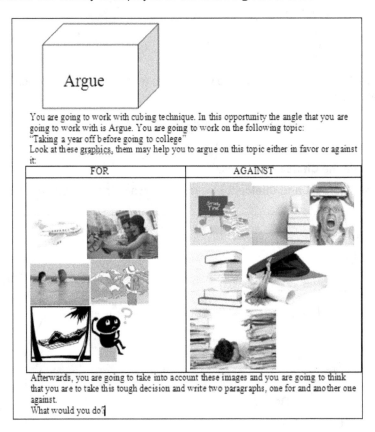

After creating the file, we are going to design the activity in our Moodle course. So follow these steps:

1. Click on **Add an activity** and select **Lesson**.

2. Complete the **Name** block.

3. We can upload a file with the description of the activity. So click on **Choose or upload a file**.

4. Click on **Upload a file**.

5. Click on **Browse**.

6. Right-click on the file and click on **Open**.

7. Click on **Upload this file**, as shown in the next screenshot:

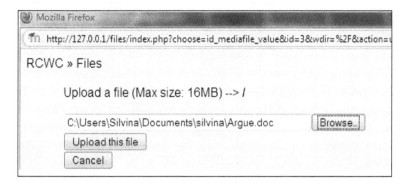

8. Check the file and click on **Choose**, as shown in the next screenshot:

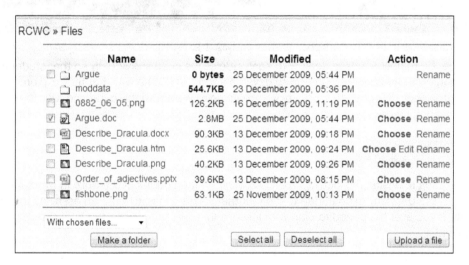

9. The file will appear in the block.

10. Click on **Save and display**.

11. Then click on **Add a question Page**.

12. Select **Essay**.

13. Complete the **Page title** and the **Page contents** and then select **Add a question page**, as shown in the next screenshot:

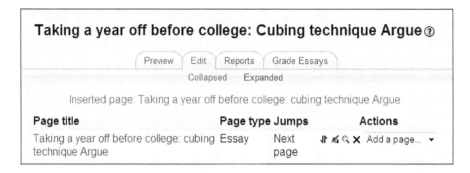

14. The activity is ready to work with!

Rolling a cube

In this recipe, students are going to write a complete essay using the six perspectives of the cube. Up to now, we have dealt with each side of the cube individually so that students can incorporate and understand how to develop a topic in such a way that they explore different aspects. Through this activity we are going to work with the cube and with the cubing technique per se.

Getting ready

We are going to design this activity in an essay within the options of the quiz. In my opinion, I think it is the best way to do it, due to the fact that students are to write an essay as the final activity. If you ever happened to plan your lessons in projects, it will be the final task. So let's Moodle it!

How to do it...

First of all, select a topic to deal with this technique. In this activity, we are going to work with **Tattoos and Piercings at School**. We are going to carry it out through an essay within the quiz options, and these are the steps you have to follow:

1. Click on **Add an activity** and select **Quiz**.

2. Complete the **Name** block.

3. Complete the **Introduction** block; you may introduce a cube showing either one angle or several angles.

4. Click on **Save and display**.

How it works...

Half of the activity is done. We have to create the essay within the quiz, so you have to follow these steps to design the activity:

1. Click on the drop-down box in **Choose** and select **Essay**.

2. Complete the **Name** block.

3. Complete the **Question text**, as shown in the next screenshot:

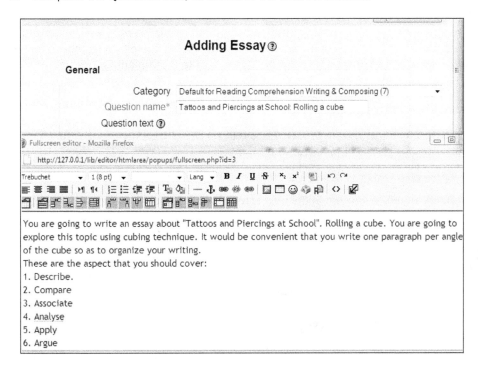

4. Click on **Save changes**.

5. Check the activity and click on **Add to quiz**.

6. Click on **Save Changes** and then click on **GO**.

7. Go back to the course as the activity is ready to work with.

How to correct this essay

In this recipe, we are going to work from another angle in our Moodle course. We are going to work as teachers. In the writing activities, we have to correct on our own. We cannot let the computer do it, and though there is a spelling corrector, we do need to check grammar, coherence, and cohesion. So let's Moodle it.

Getting ready

We have already chosen the option of the essay within the quiz, so what we can do is to write a comment on the essay of our students. We have to do it one by one; there's no other alternative to do it in a different way. We are going to write a comment for each of them.

How to do it...

We are going to change the role to teacher so that we can correct the essay. After changing the role to teacher, you have to follow these steps:

1. Click on the activity to correct.

2. Click on **Info**, as shown in the next screenshot:

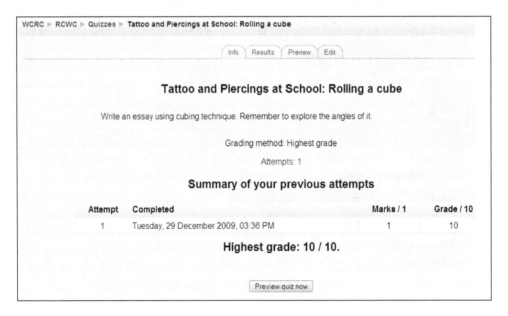

3. Click on **Results** as shown in the next screenshot:

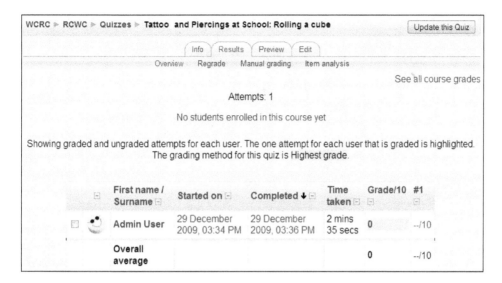

4. Then click on **0** below the **Grade** block to give a mark to the activity.

5. Click on **Make a comment or override grade**, as shown in the next screenshot:

Make comment or override grade				
History of Responses:				
# Action	Response	Time	Raw score	Grade
1 Submit	This is the essay titled Tattoos and piercings at school.	15:36:30 on 29/12/09	0	0
2 Close	This is the essay titled Tattoos and piercings at school.	15:36:41 on 29/12/09	0	0

How it works...

We have finally arrived at the block in which we can write the comment for our students. Therefore, we are going to write a comment taking into account grammar, coherence, cohesion, and usage of the cubing technique. You can also consider other aspects when correcting the essay. So these are the steps that you have to follow to write the comment:

1. Write a comment in the **Comment** block.

2. Write a grade in the **Grade** block.

3. Click on **Save**.

4. When the comment and grades are saved, it will be indicated by a window

7
Comparing using Venn Diagrams

When you hear of Venn diagrams, you may think of John Venn, the British Mathematician who invented the two or more overlapping circles used in Mathematics to show how sets relate among themselves. They are also quite useful for examining similarities and differences before writing about a certain topic. Therefore, in this chapter, we are going to deal with Venn diagrams as an activity performed before the writing process. We may give the complete Venn diagrams to our students, either before or after setting a topic so that students complete them.

As an activity performed before the writing process, it enables students to organize their writing. In other words, they will be able to organize their ideas according to their similarities or differences. A Venn diagram is very helpful to compare two or more items. Inside the circles we may use adjectives as well as words or expressions concerning comparison. The elements inside a Venn diagram are the details to be used in a comparison.

In this chapter, we will cover the following topics:

- Summer holidays versus winter holidays—drawing Venn diagrams using OpenOffice Drawing
- Living in the country versus living in an overcrowded city—drawing Venn diagrams with clip art from Microsoft Word
- Being famous versus being unknown—drawing Venn diagrams with SmartDraw software
- Having a healthy lifestyle versus bad habits—completing a Venn diagram using the website: (http://classtools.net/)
- Famous coincidences—drawing Venn diagrams of Abraham Lincoln and John Fitzgerald Kennedy using Paint

  ▶ Comparing different types of pollution—drawing Venn diagrams using Microsoft Office Visio 2007

  ▶ Types of students—drawing Venn diagrams using Edraw Max

  ▶ Puzzles—placing adjectives and sentences in a Venn diagram according to the description of personal possession

Introduction

In this chapter, you will be able to design several types of Exercises concerning writing and composing through Moodle 1.9.5 using Venn diagrams. Students can use these diagrams as a prewriting activity in order to organize their thinking. They will be able to design different types of writing. This technique can be used to compare two or more items or people, write a "for-and-against" essay, as well as state a point of view supporting ideas using facts supplied by the Venn diagram keywords.

We can design the activities in such a way that students can interact among themselves while completing the Moodle courses. Apart from that, each recipe will describe how to develop this technique in order to carry out the Venn diagram in another way, using resources from Web 2.0.

Venn diagrams are simple graphic organizers that are a very helpful tool to make it easier to write the final draft. Apart from that, through this methodology students are capable of understanding how to put data together. Students are also able to examine different types of information.

We are going to design the activities using different software such as EDraw Max, SmartDraw, Microsoft Word, OpenOffice, Visio as well as resources from Web 2.0. In this case, we are going to use the `http://classtools.net/` website where students can complete the Venn diagrams by themselves and embed it into our Moodle course. We will also design Venn diagrams with words and pictures. The addition of pictures in this type of Exercise creates a more visually rich activity, apart from the fact that students will imagine them before writing.

Summer holidays versus winter holidays—drawing Venn diagrams using OpenOffice Drawing

In this Assignment, we are going to show the students two Venn diagrams, which are going to compare two types of holidays. There are many similarities between them, though some differences exist. They will have to fill them afterwards, and they are going to write an essay titled 'Summer Holidays or Winter Holidays?'

Getting ready

Let's create the Venn diagram using the website, `http://www.openoffice.org/`. We are going to use this free and open source software in order to create the activity. We will be clicking on **Drawing** in order to draw both circles of the diagram and write titles for the activity and each diagram.

How to do it...

Click on **Drawing** in OpenOffice and then follow these steps:

1. Click on the **Basic Shapes** icon in the bottom part of the screen and select **Circle**.
2. Copy and paste another circle, and overlap it on the other one to create a Venn diagram.
3. Select one circle and click on the **Effects** icon and then click on **Transparency**, as shown in the next screenshot:

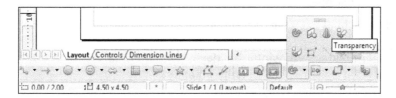

4. In order to write the title of the activity, you can use the **Fontwork Gallery**. It is the icon with an A inside a frame.
5. Write the title for each circle, as shown in the next screenshot:

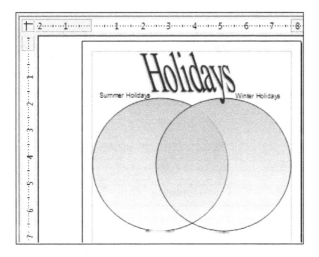

6. The activity is ready for insertion in the Moodle course.

How it works...

We are going to carry out this activity with an Exercise in our Moodle course by uploading a file giving the outlines for the activity. Students have to upload a file after the Venn diagrams are completed. Afterwards, using the information that they have written, they are going to write an essay. So they may either upload one file or two. Let's Moodle it!

Select the Weekly outline section where you want to insert the activity and follow these steps:

1. Click on **Add an activity** and select **Exercise**.

2. Complete the **Title** block. You may change the other items or leave them the way they are.

3. Click on **Save and display**.

4. Click on **Continue**.

5. Complete the **Editing Assessment Elements** blocks and click on **Save changes**.

6. Click on **Continue**.

7. Click on **Submit Exercise Description**, as shown in the next screenshot:

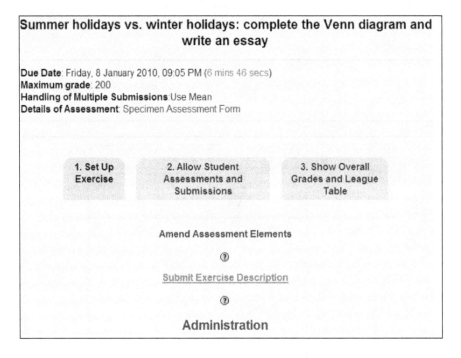

8. Click on **Browse** and select the file that you want to upload.

9. Write a **Title** in the title block.

10. Click on **Upload this file**, as shown in the next screenshot:

> ### Summer holidays vs. winter holidays: complete the Venn diagram and write an essay
>
> **Due Date**: Friday, 8 January 2010, 09:05 PM (11 mins 12 secs)
> **Maximum grade**: 200
> **Handling of Multiple Submissions**:Use Mean
> **Details of Assessment**: Specimen Assessment Form
>
> ---
>
> ### Submit Exercise Description:
>
> C:\Users\Silvina\Documents\Venn diagram holidays.o [Browse...]
> Title: [Summer holidays vs. winter holidays]
>
> [Upload this file] (Maximum upload size: 16MB)

11. Click on **Continue**.

12. Then click on **Allow Student Assessment and Submissions** so that students can submit their files.

Living in the country versus living in an overcrowded city—drawing Venn diagrams with clip art from Microsoft Word

In this recipe, we are going to design Venn diagrams with pictures for our students and we will provide labels for them to help in their writing. This activity will help us to design a visually rich activity and facilitate students to imagine themselves in future situations and how to organize their thinking in their mind's eye. So, we are going to design the Venn diagrams in Microsoft Word using clip art. Later, we will upload it into our Moodle course as a resource. So, let's get ready!

Getting ready

As I have already mentioned, we are going to draw Venn diagrams in Microsoft Word. The topic that I have chosen to deal with is "Living in the country versus living in an overcrowded city". We are not going to mention the geographical situations of such places; we will only show their pictures. In this recipe, we are going to use **Clip art on Office Online**.

How to do it...

We are going to start Microsoft Word to draw the Venn diagrams using a template, with the clip art from the website. These are the steps that you have to follow:

1. Click on **Insert** and select **SmartArt**.

2. Click on **Relationship** and select **Basic Venn**, as shown in the next screenshot:

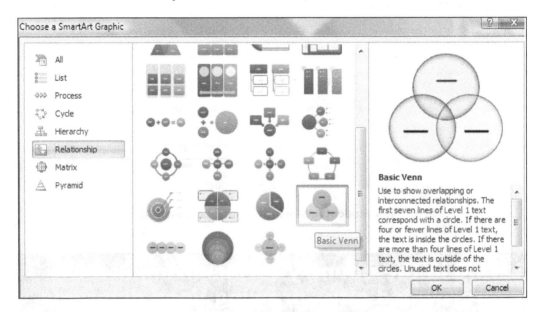

3. Click on **OK**.

4. Click on one circle in order to remove it, as shown in the next screenshot:

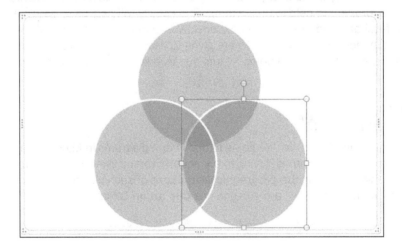

5. Press *Delete* so that we have only two circles.

6. Click on **Insert** and select **Clip art**.

7. Select **Clip art on Office Online**, as shown in the next screenshot:

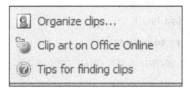

8. Complete the **Search** block to find the picture.

9. Click on the picture that you want to insert. Click on **Add to Basket** when a pop up appears.

10. Next, click on **Download**.

11. Then click on **Open with**.

12. Right click on picture, select **Copy** and paste the image to the desired position in the document.

How it works...

After creating the Venn diagrams with clip art, we will create the activity in our Moodle course. We are going to include our document as a resource and then design a writing activity where students are going to upload a single file. They may use the same file with their writing or they may create another one. So select the Weekly outline section where you want to insert the activity and follow these steps:

1. Click on **Add a resource** and select **Link to a file or website**.

2. Complete the **Name** block.

3. Complete the **Summary** block.

4. Click on **Choose or upload a file**.

5. Click on **Upload a file**.

6. Click on **Browse** and search for your file.

7. Click on **Upload this file**.

8. Click on **Choose**.

9. In **Target**, select **New window**.

10. Click on **Save and return to course**.

Now we are going to design the Assignment that we want our students to write. Follow these steps in order to create the Assignment:

1. Click on **Add an activity**, and within Assignment, select **Upload a single file**.

2. Complete the **Assignment name** block.

3. Complete the **Description** block.

4. Click on **Save and return to course**.

5. The activity appears as shown in the next screenshot:

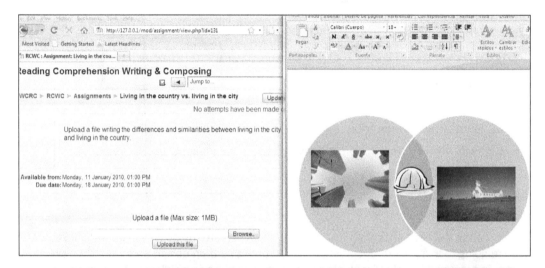

Being famous versus being unknown— drawing Venn diagrams with SmartDraw software

Do you think that the media pays too much attention to famous people's personal lives? Let's see what the opinion of our students is! In this recipe, we are going to provide students with similarities between being famous and unknown and they have to write the special characteristics of each one. We won't name these famous persons. We will allow them to describe their hero as it would be much more appealing to them.

Getting ready

We are going to use SmartDraw software. You can download a free trial from the following website: http://www.smartdraw.com. Then we will create a Venn diagram using this software and upload it into our Moodle course. Students are going to write a "for-and-against essay", but we will provide the introduction and the conclusion for this piece of writing.

How to do it...

First open SmartDraw and follow these steps:

1. Click on **Basics** and select **More**.

2. Click on the **Venn Diagram** template.

3. Click on the third circle at the bottom and press *Delete* because in this case we are working with two circles only.

4. Click on **Click to Add Text** and complete the similarities we are going to give them.

5. Save the file as `.png`, as shown in the next screenshot:

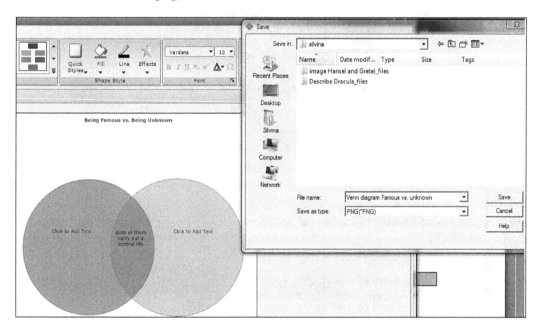

6. Complete the following chart as shown in the next screenshot:

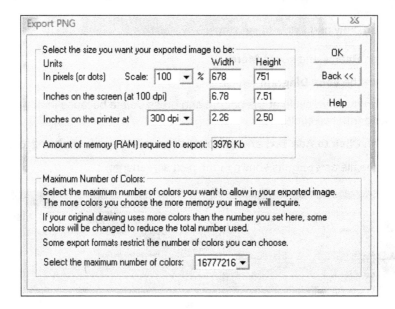

7. Click on **OK**.

How it works...

We have just created part of the activity in SmartDraw. Now we are going to design the other part of the activity. We are going to perform it in an Essay inside the Quiz option. So you have to follow these steps:

1. Select **Add an activity** and click on **Quiz**.

2. Complete the **Name** as well as the **Introduction** blocks.

3. Click on **Save and display**.

4. Complete the **Question name**.

5. Complete the **Question text**. Remember to write the introduction and the conclusion of the essay. In the **Question text**, select the Venn diagram words and click on the **Insert Web Link** icon.

6. Click on **Browse** and then on **Browse** in the next window, as shown in the next screenshot:

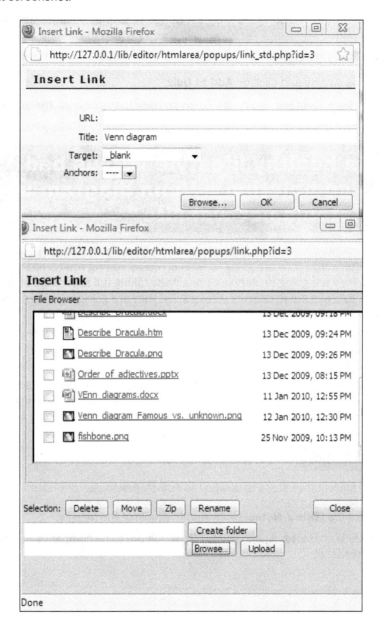

7. Search for the file that we created and click on **Open**.

8. Click on **Upload** and then click on the file's name.

9. Complete the **Insert Link** block **Title** and select **New window** in **Target**. Then click on **OK**.

10. You may choose to display the image in **Image to display** because we have saved the file as `.png`.

11. Click on **Save Changes**.

12. Check the activity and click on **Add to Quiz**.

13. Click on **Save changes** and on **Go**. Then go back to the course. The activity is ready to work with.

Having a healthy lifestyle versus bad habits—completing a Venn diagram using the classtools.net website

In this recipe, students are going to complete Venn diagrams in the `http://classtools.net/` website. Afterwards, they are going to write an essay stating what a healthy lifestyle means to them. They are going to carry out the activity taking full advantage of Web 2.0. We will create a link to a website to describe the activity. They are going to perform the writing part of the activity in an Assignment in **Online text**. So let's get ready!

Getting ready

We are going to enter the `http://classtools.net/` website and we are going to select the Venn diagram template. After choosing the template, we'll select a two circle template only. Let's see how to do it.

How to do it...

You are going to follow these steps to design the activity previously introduced:

1. Complete the **[Title / Notes]** block with the topic of the activity.

2. Complete both **[factor 1]** and **[factor 2]**, which are to be compared, as shown in the next screenshot:

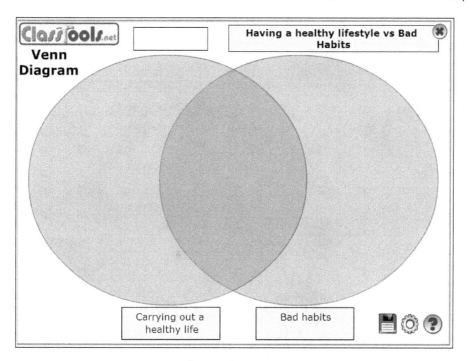

3. Click on the **Save as webpage** icon.

4. Click on **Save file**.

5. Click on **OK**.

6. Click on the **Embed into blog in the webpage** icon.

7. Select the embed code and copy it. Then click on **OK**.

How it works...

As we will be designing the rest of the activity in our Moodle course, we will select the Weekly outline section where we want to insert our activity and follow these steps:

1. Click on **Add an activity**, and within Assignments, click on **Online text**.

2. Complete the **Assignment name** block.

3. Complete the **Description** block and click on the **Toggle HTML Source** icon.

4. Paste the embed code that you have copied before. Then click on the **Toggle HTML source** icon again.

5. Click on **Save and return to course**

6. The activity appears, as shown in the next screenshot:

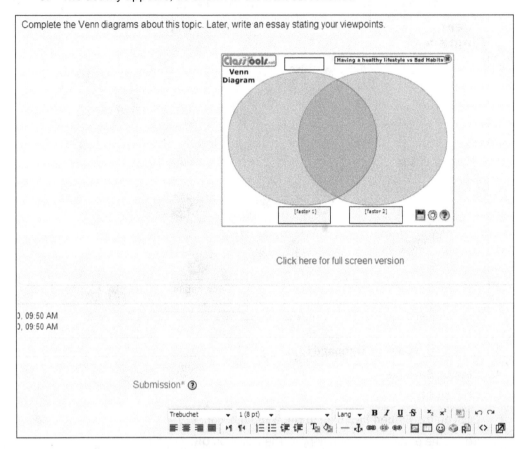

Click here for full screen version

Famous coincidences—drawing Venn diagrams of Abraham Lincoln and John Fitzgerald Kennedy using Paint

(Image credit: `http://theshadowlands.net/mystery.htm`.)

In this recipe, we are going to work with the biographies of these two USA presidents. They share many things in common apart from the fact that they were both USA presidents 100 years apart. Therefore students are going to read their biographies and complete a Venn diagram using that data. Then they are going to write an article using that information.

Getting ready

We are going to work with Paint in order to design the Venn diagram. Therefore, we will open Paint to draw the diagrams. Afterwards, we are going to carry out the activity in our Moodle course in **Advanced uploading of files** within Assignments.

How to do it...

You are going to open Paint and follow these steps to design the Venn diagrams:

1. Click on the text icon in order to write the title of the activity.

2. Click on the circle icon and draw one circle and then click on this icon again to draw another circle to complete the Venn diagram.

3. Save the file as .png. The diagram is shown in the next screenshot:

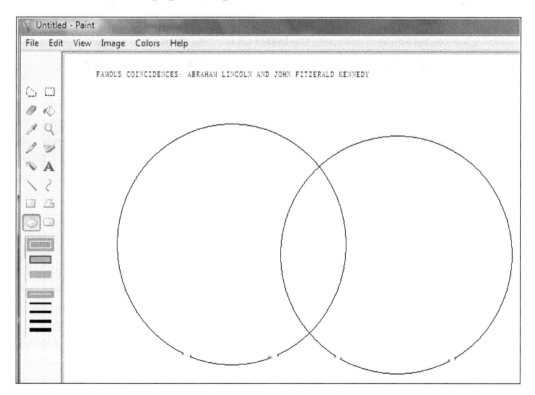

How it works...

We have only designed the Venn diagrams in Paint. Now we have to perform this activity in our Moodle course. We are going to perform the writing activity in **Advanced uploading of files** because we want our students to upload both the Venn diagrams and complete the piece of writing. Therefore, we are going to select the Weekly outline section where you want to insert the activity and these are the steps to follow:

1. Click on **Add an activity** and select **Advanced uploading of files** within Assignments.

2. Complete the **Assignment name** block.

3. Complete the **Description** block. In this case, we are going to create a link to the following websites: `http://www.whitehouse.gov/about/presidents/abrahamlincoln`, `http://www.whitehouse.gov/about/presidents/johnfkennedy` and `http://theshadowlands.net/jfk.htm`. In these three cases, complete the **Insert Link** block and select **New window**.

4. The first two websites are the biographies of the presidents and the third website describes the similarities they share between them.

5. Click on **Insert Web Link** icon, click on **Browse**, select the file you want to upload (the Venn diagram that we have created in Paint), and then click on **Open**.

6. Click on **Upload**.

7. Click on the **File** and complete the **Insert Link** block. Then click on **OK**.

8. Click on **Save and return to course** and the activity appears as shown in the next screenshot:

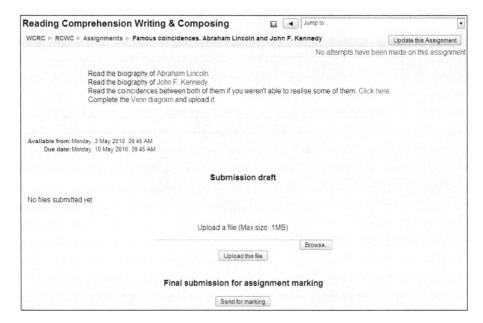

Comparing different types of pollution— drawing Venn diagrams using Microsoft Visio 2007

In this recipe, we are going to work with different types of pollution which are damaging our environment. Here we will deal with air pollution, domestic pollution, and water pollution. As we are going to deal with three types of pollution, we will work with a three circle diagram. We are going to draw the Venn diagram with Microsoft Visio 2007.

Getting ready

Open Microsoft Visio 2007. You can download a free trial of this product from the following website: `http://us20.trymicrosoftoffice.com/default.aspx?culture=en-US`. So, if you don't have the software, you can try it out and get it!

How to do it...

Before creating the activity in Moodle, we have to draw the Venn diagram in Microsoft Visio 2007. So we are going to use this software. These are the steps you have to follow:

1. Click on **File | New | New Drawing (US units)**, as shown in the next screenshot:

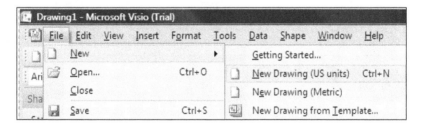

2. In the **Search for shapes** block, write the word "Venn" and click on the **arrow** key.

3. Click on the Venn diagram and it will appear on the blank document.

4. Enlarge the diagram.

5. Click on the **Text Tool** icon and write the title of the activity.

6. Label each circle with the different types of pollution to work with.

7. Right-click on the image and select **Shape | Ungroup**, as shown in the next screenshot:

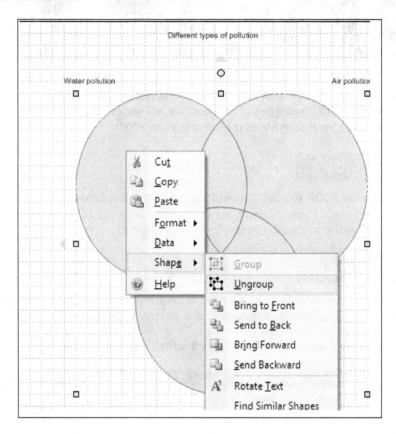

8. Click on **OK**.

9. Color each section in a different color. Click on the section to color and click on the **Fill color** icon, as shown in the next screenshot:

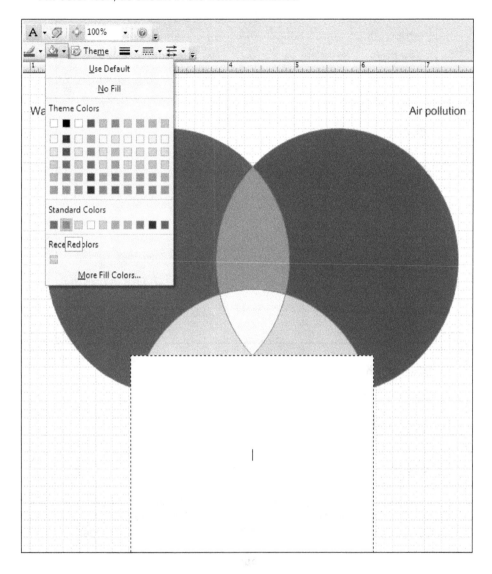

10. Choose the color you want.

11. Save the image. Click on **File | Save as** and write a name for the file. Save it as `.png` extension. Click on **Save**.

12. Complete the following block, as shown in the next screenshot:

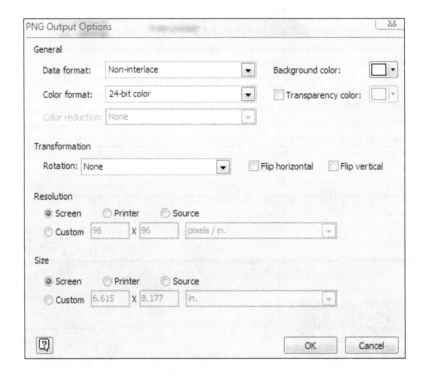

13. Then click on **OK**.

The graphic of the Venn diagram is ready.

How it works...

We have just created our Venn diagram using Microsoft Visio 2007. Now we are going to upload the image to our Moodle course and create three links to websites which describe the different types of pollution. We are going to select the Weekly outline section where you want to carry out the activity and design this activity in a Journal. It is a very good option to carry out this kind of activity, though you may select another option. Follow these steps:

1. Click on **Add an activity** and select **Journal**.

2. Complete the **Journal name**.

3. Complete the **Journal question** and write the description of the activity. We are going to create links to the following websites: http://www.sciencedaily.com/articles/w/water_pollution.htm, http://www.sciencedaily.com/articles/earth_climate/air_pollution/, and http://www.whoi.edu/page.do?pid=12469. In each case, complete the **Insert Link** block and select **New window** in **Target**. These are examples; you may choose other websites.

4. To upload the Venn diagram, click on the icon to insert a picture.
5. Click on **Browse** to find the file.
6. When you have found the file, click on **Open.**
7. Copy and paste the link that appears at the bottom of the screen in the **Image URL block.**
8. Complete the **Alternate text block.**
9. Click on **Upload.**
10. Click on the file that you just uploaded and then click on **OK.**
11. The activity is shown in the next screenshot:

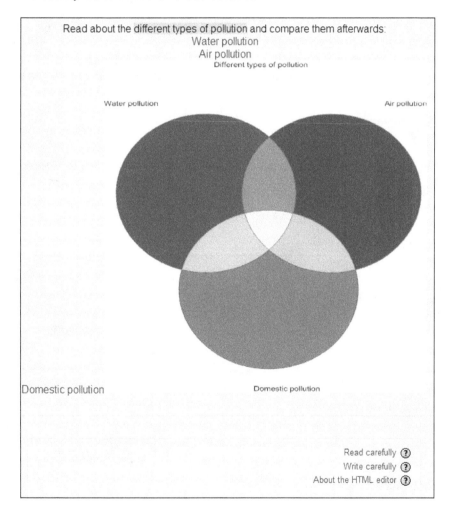

Read about the different types of pollution and compare them afterwards:
Water pollution
Air pollution
Different types of pollution

Water pollution

Air pollution

Domestic pollution

Domestic pollution

Read carefully ⑦
Write carefully ⑦
About the HTML editor ⑦

Types of students—drawing Venn diagrams using Edraw Max

We are going to add social material in this recipe because we are going to create a Wiki and upload a Venn diagram from Edraw Max to our Moodle course. We have already used this software in other recipes. You can download a free trial from this website: `http://www.edrawsoft.com/download.php`.

Getting ready

We will design the Venn diagram in the previously mentioned software and compare the different types of students: great students, passing students, and lazy ones. We are going to do it through a workshop because they are going to think about themselves and write the characteristics of each one. Apart from that, they can label themselves according to their way of studying.

How to do it...

Start Edraw Max, and to create the diagram, these are the steps you have to follow:

1. Click on **Home | Business diagram**.

2. Select the **Charts and Graphs** template, which contains the Venn diagram, as shown in the next screenshot:

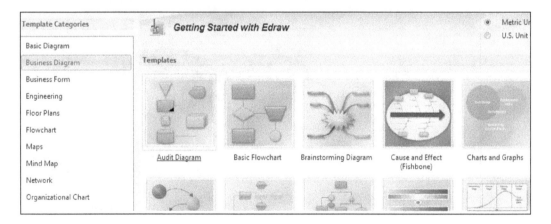

3. Drag and drop the three circle Venn diagram to the drawing page.

4. Write a title and label each circle with the types of students that we have already mentioned. Click on the **Text Tool** icon and draw a rectangle in the document in order to write the text, as shown in the following screenshot:

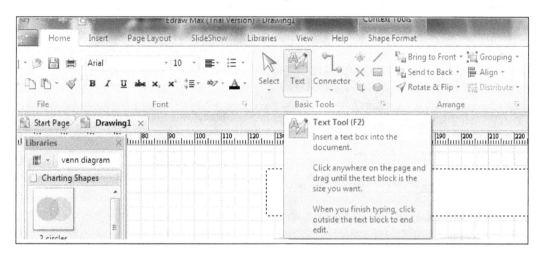

5. Click on the disk icon in order to save it.
6. Name the file and then click on **Save**.

How it works...

Part of the activity is done. What we have to do now is upload this activity in Moodle and let our students think and write. As we have already mentioned, we are going to create a Wiki so that students can interact and write specific characteristics about themselves. Afterwards, they have to write an article about different types of students. Select the Weekly outline section where you want to place the activity and these are the steps that you need to follow so as to design this activity. Let's Moodle it!

1. Click on **Add an activity** and select **Wiki**.
2. Complete the **Summary** block.
3. Select the words Venn diagram and click on the **Insert Web Link** icon.
4. Click on **Browse** and then click on **Browse** again.
5. Look for your file and click on **Open**.
6. Click on **Upload**.
7. Double click on the file.
8. Complete the **Title** block.
9. Select **New window** in **Target**.

10. Click on **OK**.

11. Click on **Save and return to course**.

12. The activity appears as shown in the next screenshot:

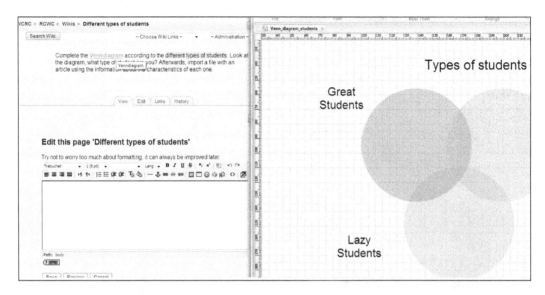

Puzzles—placing adjectives and sentences in a Venn diagram according to the description of personal possessions

This is a very simple recipe because it is the final one, and apart from that, we have worked with several ways of drawing Venn diagram as well as topics. It is high time for our students to do it by themselves. The purpose of this recipe is to increase and enhance the vocabulary of our students. Later they may write an article about it.

Getting ready

The topic of this recipe has to do with the possessions of students—their pet, town, and friends. It will be a puzzle because we are going to provide some words or sentences that they have to place somewhere in the Venn diagrams. They have to add others as well. It would be a good idea to include words that our students do not generally use. So let's Moodle it!

How to do it...

After selecting the Weekly outline section where you want to display the activity, you are going to follow these steps:

1. Click on **Add an activity**, and within Assignments, select **Offline activity**.
2. Complete the **Assignment name** block.
3. Then complete the **Description** block with the description of the activity by adding the words and sentences that you want your students to work with.
4. Then click on **Save and return to course**.

How it works...

When your students click on the activity, they will have to draw the Venn diagram and use the words, phrases, or sentences that we have written in the activity. Afterwards, they have to write an article using the information in the Venn diagram and the data that we have given them.

8
Composing New Sceneries

Have you ever thought of changing something to improve it? If the answer to this question is "No", it would be a good idea to take a look at these recipes! It is sometimes easier for our students to change things that already exist instead of inventing new ones. Therefore, it is an interesting option in this chapter to search for different ways of changing things in order to recreate them. This chapter tries to rebuild things that already exist, but by twisting them in such a way that students are going to create something new on their own. They will be guided to perform a passive activity before the writing one because they will have to read before writing.

In this chapter, we will cover the following topics:

- Updating a fairy tale—using a database to guide writing activity
- Changing a poem into a cartoon—using resources from Web 2.0
- Listening to a poem and writing another end to it
- Imagining that your house is a palace
- Superheroes have other powers—creating your own hero using tools from Web 2.0
- Flying shoes—creating an Ad using the website (`http://animoto.com/`)
- Becoming your idol—using Quandary 2 in Moodle
- Embedding a video from YouTube and changing the lyrics of the song

Introduction

In this chapter, you will be taking full advantage of the many resources that Web 2.0 offers currently. The activities are funny and out of the blue to broaden students' creativity. If we want to enhance the thinking of our students, we have to make them think of something that they do not cope with every day. So these are the activities for them to create. The activities are very simple because they are going to interact with somebody's work. We are going to help them brighten their imagination through the entertaining recipes later in this chapter.

Teaching the art of writing involves teaching creativity as well. So we have to teach our students how to explore that field. In this case, we are dealing with recreating or guiding them through the result of a piece of writing by setting procedures, which they have to focus on.

The recipes are designed in such a way that students are going to find them attractive, though you may change some of them or part of them using your own creativity.

In this virtual classroom, we are going to enrich the use of Web 2.0 resources as mentioned previously. Students will be much more attracted to the activities. Later the writing part of each activity will appear.

Updating a fairy tale—using a database to guide writing activity

In this task, we are going to use some information from a fairy tale that students should all know, and they are going to change it by adding items from our society. These items could be mainly technological. We are to focus on rewriting what has been written by a famous writer, change the end, or change the plot of the story. This is because if students add something different to the story, they would be changing the general idea of it. The fairy tale that I suggest in this case is *Rapunzel*; you may choose another one or you may even choose a story that you have been dealing with. I propose to do this task through Moodle.

Getting ready

Before developing the activity in our Moodle course, we are going to surf the web and look for a website that tells Rapunzel's story. Although it may seem childish, students have the option to read it or not. It would be interesting for them to read it because they have to rewrite the story and they have to insert the updating elements in it afterwards. Apart from that, they need to read before writing because they can take many ideas and vocabulary from this passive activity.

How to do it...

We are going to carry out this activity in two parts. The first part is going to be a database because we are going to guide students to think and answer some questions before inserting the new elements in the story. After that they are going to perform the writing task in a Journal. So enter the course and choose the Weekly outline section where you want to insert the activity and follow these steps:

1. Click on the drop-down box in **Add an activity** and select **Database**.

2. Complete the **Name** block.

3. Complete the **Introduction** block and create a link to a website that retells *Rapunzel's* story. These are the ones that I have chosen: `http://www.eastoftheweb.com/ short-stories/UBooks/Rapu.shtml` and `http://www.childrenstory. info/childrenstories/rapunzel.html?cPath=52`. The first one is longer than the second one, but you can listen to the story in the latter.

4. Click on **Save and display**.

5. Click on the drop-down box and select **Text**, as shown in the next screenshot:

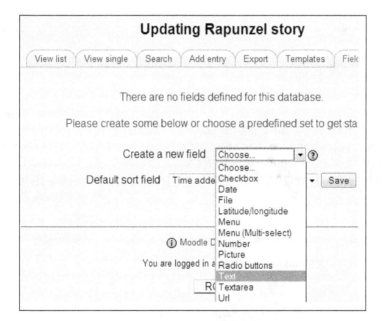

6. Complete the **Field name** block adding questions to guide the students to choose the elements that they want to add along with the reason.

7. Click on **Add**.

8. Then click on **Save**, as shown in the following screenshot:

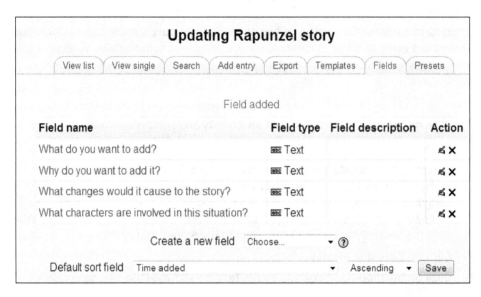

9. Click on **Continue** and go back to the course. The database is ready for your students to work with!

How it works...

The first part of the activity is a passive one, which is reading the story. It would be great if students read both stories in the aforementioned websites because they are two different versions and this would enhance their vocabulary through reading. Afterwards, they have to answer the questions in the database, which are not reading comprehension ones, but they will lead a path to what they are going to write afterwards. So, now we are going to design a Journal and they are going to use the information in the database to change the story. Follow these steps:

1. Click on **Add an activity** and select **Journal**.

2. Complete the **Journal name**.

3. Fill the **Journal question**, as shown in the next screenshot:

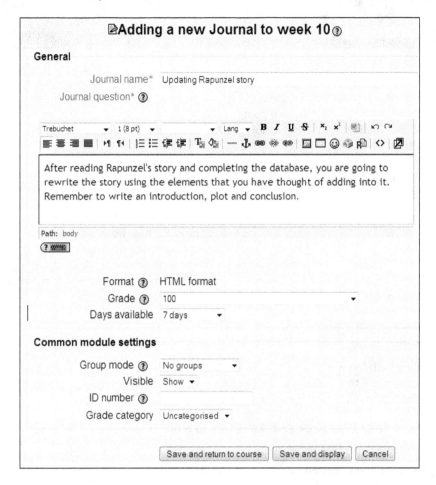

4. Click on **Save and return to course**.

Changing a poem into a cartoon—using resources from Web 2.0

In this recipe, you are going to provide students with a poem to be changed into a cartoon. It will be a great activity because you will have different versions of the same poem changed into a cartoon. It is a great way for them to explore another way of writing because cartoons are a way of writing dialogues. We are going to divide the activity in two parts as done in the previous recipe. The first part is the reading of the poem and the second one is the writing of the comic strip.

Getting ready

First, we have to choose the website where we want our students to read the poem. In previous chapters, we have already worked with poems. So now we are going to use a different website. In this case, I found a very interesting website devoted to Christmas, which provides Christmas carols, Christmas songs, and Christmas poems. I have chosen a poem by Clement Clarke Moore called *Twas the Night before Christmas*. You are free to select any other poem or piece of writing that you want your students to turn into a cartoon.

How to do it...

After selecting both the website and the poem that we want our students to work with, we are going to create a link to a website so that students can read the poem. To perform this activity in a very simple and quick way, these are the steps that you have to follow:

1. Click on **Add a resource** and select **Link to a file or web site**.
2. Complete the **Name** block.
3. Complete the **Location** block inside **Link to a file or web site**. In this case, the URL is `http://www.carols.org.uk/twas_the_night_before_christmas.htm`.

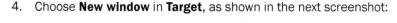
4. Choose **New window** in **Target**, as shown in the next screenshot:

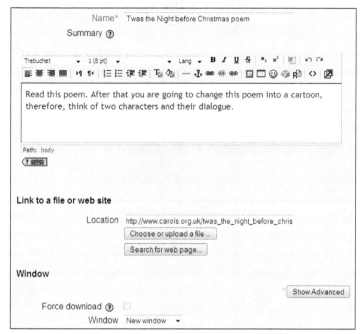

5. Click on **Save and return to course**.

How it works...

After creating the link to the website, we are going to ask our students to change the poem into a cartoon. Therefore, we can provide them with powerful tools from our beloved Web 2.0, which caters for a variety of ways to do so. We are going to develop this activity in **Offline activity** within Assignments so that students can design it. And they would feel more comfortable with its usage. They can even draw a comic strip with Microsoft Word or OpenOffice as we have already designed in earlier chapters. So let's Moodle it.

These are the steps that you have to follow:

1. Click on **Add an activity** and select **Offline activity** within Assignments.

2. Complete the **Assignment name** block.

3. Complete the **Description** block and create the links to the websites as shown in the following screenshots:

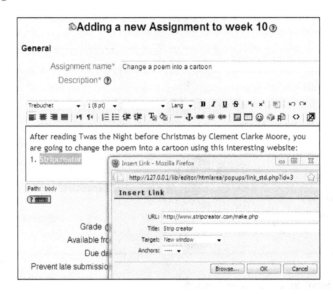

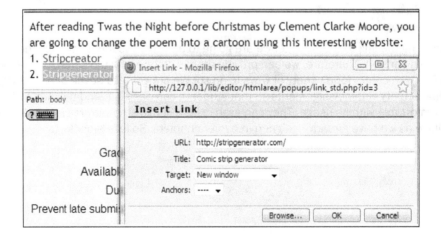

4. In both cases, click on **OK** and select **New window** in **Target**.

5. Click on **Save and return to course**. The activity is ready for your students to work with!

There's more...

Students may "cartoonize" themselves and insert their cartoonized picture in the comic strip. There are several websites that can be used for this purpose. Some websites ask you to pay in order to get the cartoonized picture. In others, you can have it freely created.

Cartoonizing ourselves

Enter the following website: `http://www.befunky.com/` and click on **Get Started**. Next, click on **Create** and select **Photo effects**. Then browse for the picture that you want to cartoonize or add effects and upload it. In the next screenshot, I have chosen the second effect. There are some effects that have to be paid for, though others are free. The following screenshot shows what you can do with a picture:

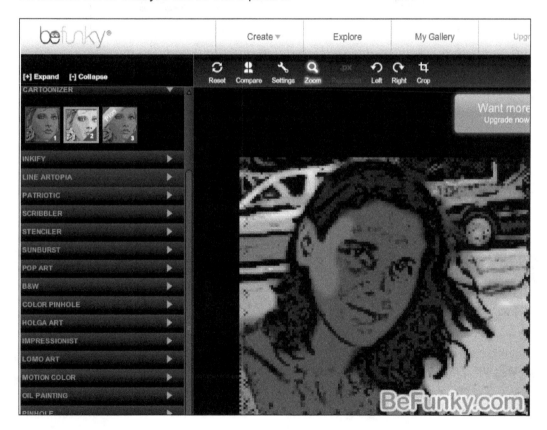

Cartoonizing ourselves using Photo to Cartoon

The following software is another tool available to convert photos to cartoons. You can download a free trial from `http://www.caricaturesoft.com/download.html`. The photo will appear as shown in the following screenshot:

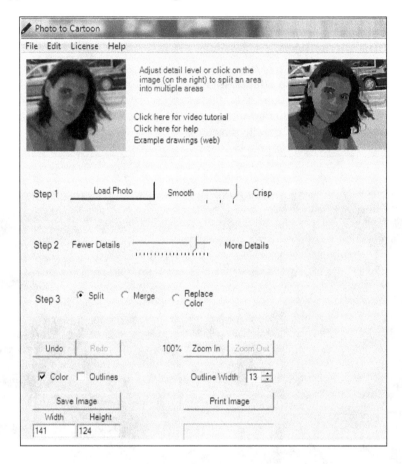

The image on the left is the picture and the image on the right is my cartoonized picture! I did not change the settings much. There is a tutorial that leads you through how to change the image, though only the three steps indicated before are necessary to do it.

Listening to a poem and writing another end to it

In this recipe, we are going to add some sound to the course. Reading a poem is not the same as listening to it because of the stress on the words, and apart from that, we can listen to somebody else reading it aloud for us. Therefore, my proposal for this activity is to listen to a poem and, as the title says, write a different end.

Getting ready

Take into account that this is a very simple recipe, so the steps to be followed are very simple. There are several websites that provide different poems and many of them are recorded. We are going to create a link to a website in order to listen to the poem. Another possibility is that you read the poem, record it, and upload it to the Moodle course. So let's Moodle it!

How to do it...

We are going to surf the Internet and look for an interesting website that has poems and where poems are recorded. Then we are going to enter the course and select the Weekly outline section where we want to add this activity so that we can design it. Afterwards, you are going to follow these steps:

1. Click on **Add a resource** and select **Link to a file or web site**.
2. Fill the **Name** block.
3. Then complete the **Location** block with the following URL: `http://www.poets.org/viewmedia.php/prmMID/20770`. The website appears as shown in the next screenshot (students cannot read the poem, they can only listen to it):

4. In the **Target** block, select **New window**.

5. Click on **Save and return to course**.

How it works...

After listening to the poem, students will write another end to it. Therefore, we are going to design the active part of the activity. In this case, we can use **Online text**, so these are the steps you need to follow:

1. Click on **Add an activity** and select **Online text** within Assignments.

2. Complete the **Assignment name** block.

3. Complete the **Description** block, as shown in the next screenshot:

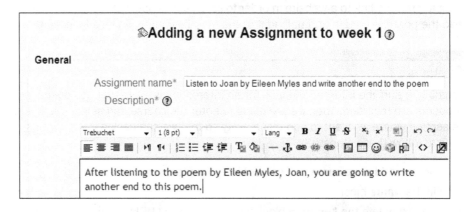

4. Click on **Save and return to course**.

Imagining that your house is a palace

In this recipe, we are going to imagine that something unusual belongs to our students, unless the children of any king or queen are our students! Apart from that, students can think backwards in time. They may imagine how life would have been centuries ago, or they may think about how their lives would be in the Web 2.0 era when living in a castle.

Getting ready

We are going to design a Wiki activity to introduce some social interaction in this chapter. First of all, we are going to surf the net to select a website that gives extra data to our students about castles. Let's Moodle it!

How to do it...

We are going to enter the Weekly outline section where we want to add the activity. Then, these are the steps that you have to follow:

1. Click on **Add an activity** and select **Forum**.

2. Complete the **Forum name** block.

3. Click on the drop-down box in **Forum type** and select **Q and A forum** so that students interact among themselves, as shown in the next screenshot.

4. Complete the **Forum introduction**.

5. Create a link to a website where you can find pictures of a castle, as shown in the following screenshot:

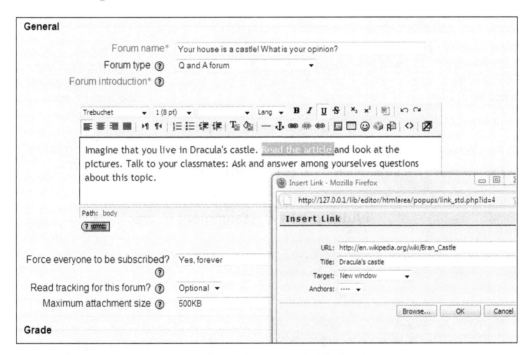

6. In **Target**, select **New window**. Then click on **OK**.

7. Click on **Save and return to course**.

8. The next screenshot shows how the Forum looks when your students interact among themselves:

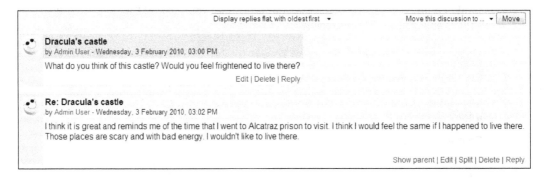

How it works...

The prewriting part is ready and students will perform two types of activities before writing—they will read an article about castles and they will discuss it. Therefore, this Forum activity is like a brainstorming activity and hence it is high time for them to write! We are going to add an Assignment so that they can write about living in a castle. Follow these steps:

1. Click on **Add an activity** and select **Upload a single file.**

2. Complete the **Assignment name** block.

3. Complete the **Description** block, as shown in the next screenshot:

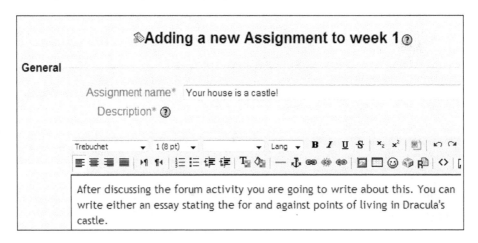

4. Click on **Save and return to course**.

Superheroes have other powers—creating your own hero using tools from Web 2.0

Have you ever wondered what powers Superman might have had if he could never fly? What about our students? What do they think about this? Why don't we ask them?

In this recipe, we are going to change Superman's powers. We are going to ask students what power instead of flying he would have. Afterwards, they can design their own hero in an interesting website. The writing activity will be profitable for our students as they will learn a lot out of this. Let's get ready!

Getting ready

We will be creating a new hero if Superman cannot fly. He is characterized because of his flying ability, apart from a cloak that is part of his costume. Taking away a power means changing his costume. This is the reason that students are going to create a new hero later with new powers using a website. Don't waste more time. Let's Moodle it!

How to do it...

We are going to add social material to this course. In this recipe, we are going to use chat so that students can interact among themselves and talk about the crazy idea of Superman losing his flying ability. So these are the steps to follow:

1. Click on **Add an activity** and select **Chat**.
2. Complete the **Name of this chat room** block.
3. Complete the **Introduction text** block.

4. Create a link to a website for more data about Superman, as shown in the next screenshot:

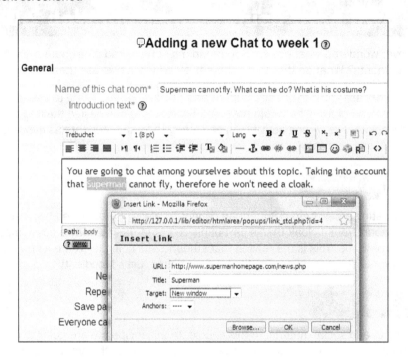

5. Select **New window** in **Target** and then click on **OK**.
6. Click on **Save and return to course**.

How it works...

After chatting among themselves, students get many ideas of the new powers of Superman. As in the previous recipe, they read an article about Superman and discuss the topic. The next activity is to read about the new Superman and write about him. We are going to design the activity in Assignment within **Advanced uploading of files**. These are the steps to follow:

1. Click on **Add an activity** and select **Advanced uploading of files**.
2. Complete the **Assignment name** block.
3. Complete the **Description** block.

4. Choose **2** in **Maximum number of uploaded files**, as shown in the next screenshot:

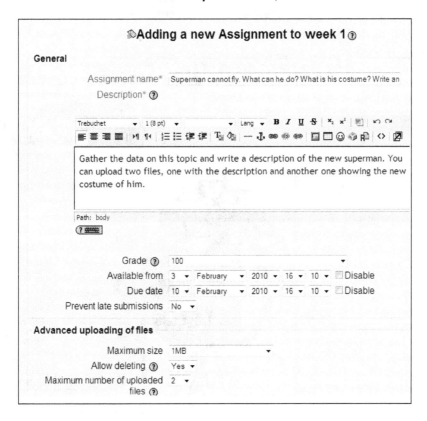

5. Click on **Save and return to course**.

There's more...

You can design another activity—for example, an **Advanced Uploading of files** within Assignments, where students can create their own hero using resources from Web 2.0. Students can upload the description as well as the image of their hero.

Writing about a hero designed using a link to a website

You can create a link to a website where students can create their hero. You can create a creature as shown in the next screenshot:

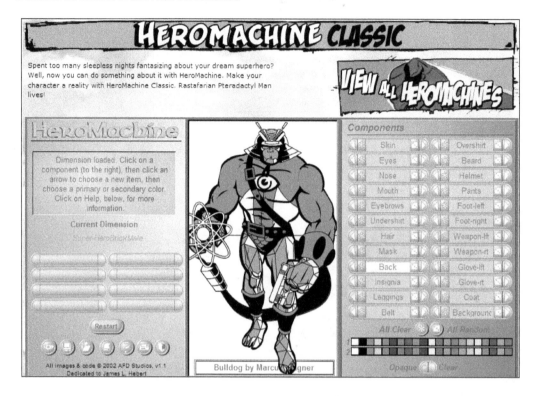

(Image credit: `http://www.ugo.com/channels/comics/heroMachine/classic.asp`)

Click on the **Restart** button and then click on the other items in order to design your hero using **Heromachine**. Follow the instructions and then click on the **Save** icon.

Flying shoes—creating an advertisement using animoto.com

Have you ever thought of having flying shoes when you are going to be late? Have you ever wanted to be in two distant places and knew that you wouldn't be able to get there on time? Whenever one of those things happened to me, I always wanted to have flying shoes. Therefore, let's see what our students think of them. It is up to us how well we can sell them! We are going to create an Ad using `http://animoto.com/`, a creative tool from our beloved Web 2.0. You can also use Microsoft PowerPoint to slideshow an Ad, though this tool is quite interesting!

Getting ready

We are going to design an Ad using the website mentioned earlier. Before entering this website, we have to select some images, music, or short videos in order to upload them to this website and create the Ad.

Afterwards, we are going to create a link to the website. Later, our students are going to use Wiki and state their opinion on the Ad. Another option is to write an article about the usage of the flying shoes, they may support the idea or oppose it. They may also write a "for-and-against" essay so that they can state their viewpoints on the subject.

How to do it...

Before creating the activity in Moodle, we have to create the Ad using Animoto.com. Therefore, we have to enter the following website: `http://animoto.com/`. First of all, you sign in and then you have to follow these steps:

1. Click on **Create video**, as shown in the next screenshot:

2. Choose your video type—they do not have a commercial type, but we can adjust the **Pandora's Gift Box**, as shown in the next screenshot:

3. Click on **Pandora's Gift Box**, then click on **free** or you may **Purchase Greeting**, as shown in the next screenshot:

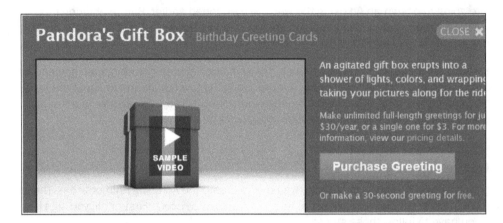

4. Follow these three steps, as shown on the left-hand side in the next screenshot:

5. After you finish designing the Ad, you will get an e-mail so that you can play the video.

6. Play the video and copy the URL to create a link to the website in our Moodle course.

How it works...

Choose the Weekly outline section where you want to carry out the activity. Design this activity in a Wiki because we want students to share the comments on this Ad. Therefore, you have to follow these steps:

1. Click on **Add an activity** and select **Wiki**.

2. Complete the **Name** block.

3. Complete the **Summary** block.

4. Create a link to the website, which shows your Ad created in `http://animoto.com/` as shown in the next screenshot:

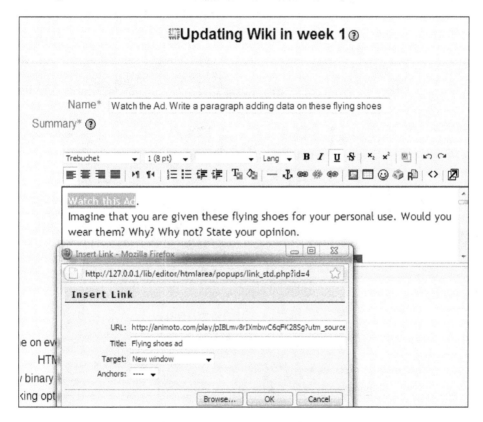

5. Complete the **Insert Link** block, as shown in the previous screenshot, then click on **OK**.

6. Click on **Save and return to course**.

Becoming your idol—using Quandary 2 in Moodle

In this recipe, students are going to use Quandary 2, which is free and open source software. They are going to imagine that every day when they get up they are another person. The best way to do it is through Quandary 2. Afterwards, we are going to upload it in Moodle as if it were a Hot Potatoes Quiz because they are the same creators.

Getting ready

You can download Quandary 2 from the following website: `http://www.halfbakedsoftware.com/quandary.php`, as shown in the next screenshot:

Click on **download page** and follow the instructions to download the software. After that, you can register for free and have much more benefits.

How to do it...

First of all, we are going to create the Quandary maze that we want our students to go through. In this case, they are going to be a different person each day. You are going to enter as many decision points as you want; but in this case, we are going to create only three. These are the steps that you have to follow:

1. Click on **File** and select **New**.
2. Complete the **Exercise Title** box.
3. Complete the **Decision Point title** box.
4. Complete the **Decision Point contents** box, as shown in the next screenshot:

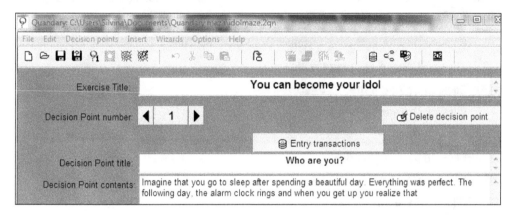

5. Click on **New Link** and click on the drop-down box in the pop-out window and select **Create a new decision point**, as shown in the next screenshot:

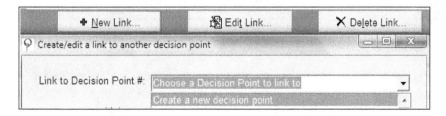

6. Complete the new box, as shown in the following screenshot:

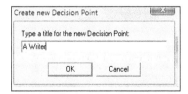

7. Click on **OK** in this block and in the previous pop-out window as well. Insert two more **New Links** in the same way.

8. Click on the right arrow on the left-hand side of margin and the number changes to number 2. Go over the same process making the maze, guiding students how they would spend their day.

9. When you finish, click on **File | Save File**.

10. Click on **File** and select **Export to XHTML**.

How it works...

It is time to upload the Quandary activity into Moodle. Therefore, select the Weekly outline section where you want to place the activity and follow these steps:

1. Click on **Add an activity** and select **Hot Potatoes Quiz**.

2. Click on **Choose or upload a file**.

3. Click on **Upload a file**.

4. Click on **Browse** and look for your file.

5. Click on **Open**.

6. Click on **Upload this file**.

7. Click on **Choose**.

8. Click on **Save and return to course**.

The activity appears as shown in the next screenshot:

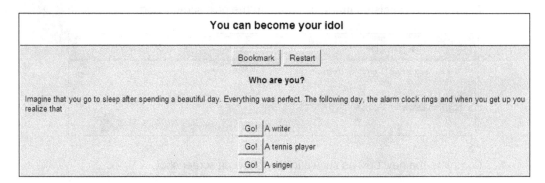

There's more...

After students have gone through the Quandary activity, we are going to create a writing one. The prewriting activity concerns using the information in the maze. In this case, this activity is both passive and active due to the fact that they have to read and then choose the next step.

Creating a writing activity

We can create a writing activity so that students can retell what happened to them when they became their idols. Therefore, you can design an **Online text** activity within Assignments.

Embed a video from YouTube and change the lyrics of the song. This is a very simple recipe. We are going to choose an official video of a musician from YouTube and embed it in our Moodle course. Students will have to change the lyrics of the song because it is another way of writing.

Getting ready

We are going to enter `http://www.youtube.com/` and then choose a video that you want to share with your students. It may be a song dealing with the description of a city—for example, old songs describing a city or a situation in which the melody is soft so that students can get inspired.

How to do it...

After choosing the Weekly outline section in which you want to display the activity, follow these steps:

1. Click on **Add an activity** and select **Journal**.

2. Complete the **Journal name** block.

3. Complete the **Journal question** block.

4. Copy the embed code in `http://www.youtube.com/`, as shown in the next screenshot:

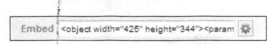

5. Click on the **Toggle HTML Source** icon and paste the code in the **Journal question** block to embed the video, as shown in the next screenshot:

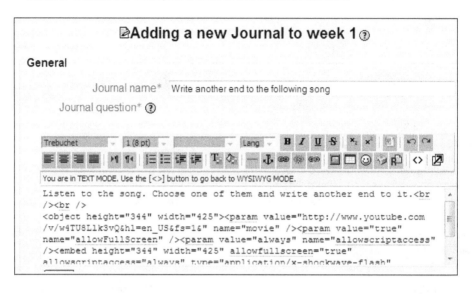

6. Click on the **Toggle HTML Source** icon again.
7. Click on **Save and return to course**.

How it works...

When your students click on the activity, it will appear as shown in the next screenshot:

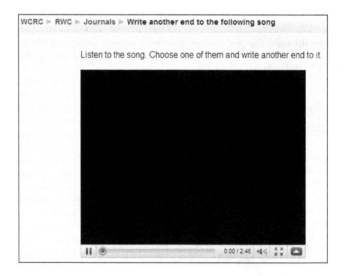

9
Working with Mind Maps and Tree Diagrams

Mind maps and tree diagrams are great techniques that can be used as prewriting activities in order to gather and organize all the information before the final piece of writing. These techniques share characteristics in that they belong to the business world, but they also adjust to education. Both are graphic techniques with a central keyword from which secondary ideas are connected.

The mind mapping technique was created by the British psychologist, Tony Buzan. You can read Tony Buzan's profile in this link, `http://www.mind-mapping.co.uk/tony-buzan-biog.htm`. A mind map is a tool that helps us to organize thoughts in a non-linear way. The advantages of using mind maps as prewriting activities are that you can facilitate the use of the right hemisphere of the brain, stimulate creativity, provide a global view, and foster the association of ideas.

Tree diagrams are used to differentiate between two things, so you can use either vocabulary or linking words to contrast two things, people, or ideas. There are two ways to draw a tree diagram, that is to say that the diagram may be horizontal or vertical, and in both cases differences are displayed.

Using tree diagrams could be considered the opposite of using Venn diagrams because when we develop a Venn diagram, we want to show similarities despite the differences among the items to be compared.

In this chapter, we will cover the following topics:

- ▶ Pictures in mind maps—using Buzan's iMindMap V4
- ▶ Adding data to pictures—creating a mind map using MindMeister
- ▶ Providing a situation to a story—drawing a mind map using the website, Draw Anywhere
- ▶ Creating mind maps using resources from Web 2.0
- ▶ Creating a tree diagram using Microsoft Word
- ▶ Pictures in a tree diagram—creating a tree diagram using the website, `creately.com`
- ▶ Completing a tree diagram comparing two persons using the website, `my.lovelycharts.com`
- ▶ Comparing the Flintstones and the Simpsons—using `cacoo.com` to create a tree diagram

Introduction

In this chapter, we are going to design four mind maps and four tree diagrams. In each recipe, we are going to use different software in order to create those graphs. After that, we are going to upload them into our Moodle course. We are going to use either commercial software or free and open source software.

In this virtual classroom, we are going to enrich the use of vocabulary, because in the creation of these techniques we have to use keywords, which have to be used in a piece of writing.

First of all, we are going to work with mind maps and then with tree diagrams. Mind maps are going to be designed according to the facilities that the different software provides us to exploit them.

Tree diagrams can be used to compare two items; therefore, in this case you are free to use either tree diagrams or Venn diagrams, which are also used to compare things. Thus, your students will choose which tool to use when they have to use a comparison text. There are two ways to design tree diagrams—either horizontal or vertical.

Pictures in mind maps—using Buzan's iMindMap V4

In this task, we are going to use the software of the inventor of mind maps: Buzan's iMindMap V4. We are going to work on the topic of robots and afterwards students are going to write an article about them. We are going to provide students with images of different robots, taking into account that a robot is not a silver rectangular human look-alike. They may have several shapes and can be used for different purposes.

Read the next screenshot, which is taken from Buzan's iMindMap V4 software, about inserting images in a mind map:

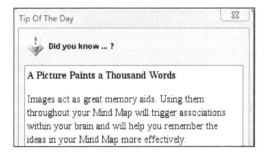

Getting ready

Let's create a mind map related to robots with pictures. After creating the mind map, students are going to look at it and they are going to write an article about the topic. In this case, the mind map will be designed with images only so as to "trigger associations within the brain" of our students. You can download a free trial of this software from the following webpage: `http://www.thinkbuzan.com/uk/`.

How to do it...

After downloading the free trial (you may also buy the software), create a new file. Then follow these steps to create a mind map with images using the previously mentioned software:

1. Choose a central image in order to write the name of the topic in the middle, as shown in the next screenshot:

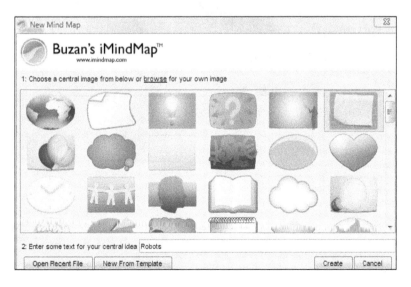

2. In **Enter some text for your central idea**, enter **Robots** as shown in the previous screenshot and click on **Create**.

3. Click on **Draw** and select **Organic**, and draw the lines of the mind map, as shown in the following screenshot:

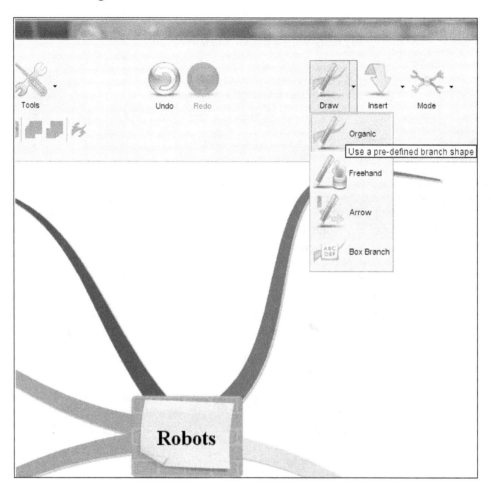

4. To add images to the mind map, click on **Insert** and select **Floating image**, as shown in the next screenshot:

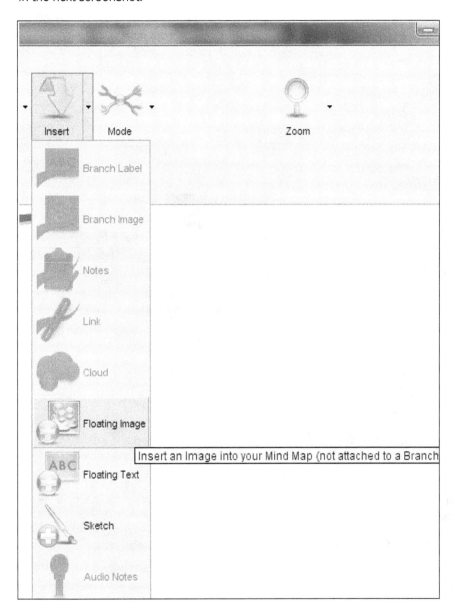

5.   Click on **View** and select **Image Library** and search for images, as shown in the next screenshot:

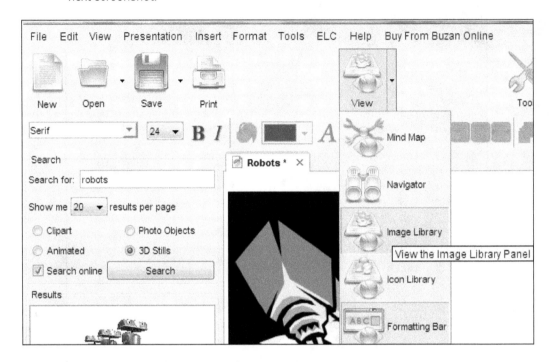

6.   Another option is to look for an image in Microsoft Word and copy and paste the images in the mind map.

7.   Save the file.

How it works...

We are going to select the Weekly outline section where we want to insert the activity. Then we are going to create a link to a file. Later, we will ask students to upload a single file in order to carry out the writing activity. Follow these steps:

1.   Click on **Add a resource** and select **Link to a file or website**.

2.   Complete the **Name** block.

3.   Complete the **Summary** block.

4.   Click on **Choose or upload a file**.

5.   Click on **Upload a file**.

6. Click on **Browse** and search for the file, then click on **Open**.

7. Click on **Upload this file** and then select **Choose**.

8. In the **Target** block, select **New window**.

9. Click on **Save and return to course**. The mind map appears as shown in following screenshot:

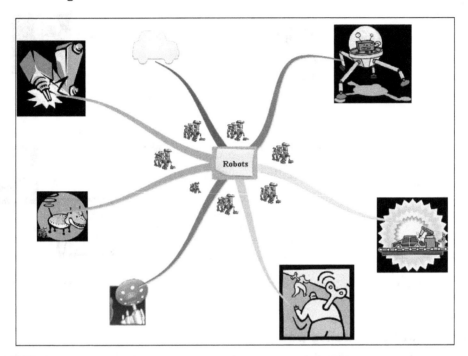

There's more...

We saw how to create a mind map related to robots previously; now we will see how to upload this mind map as an image in your course.

Uploading the mind map as .png file

If your students do not have this software and they cannot open this file, you may upload this mind map in the Moodle course as an image. These are the steps that you have to follow:

1. Open the file and fit the mind map in the screen. Press the _Prt Scr_ key.

2. Paste (_Ctrl + V_) the image in Paint or Inkscape (or any similar software).

3. Select the section of the mind map only, as shown in the next screenshot:

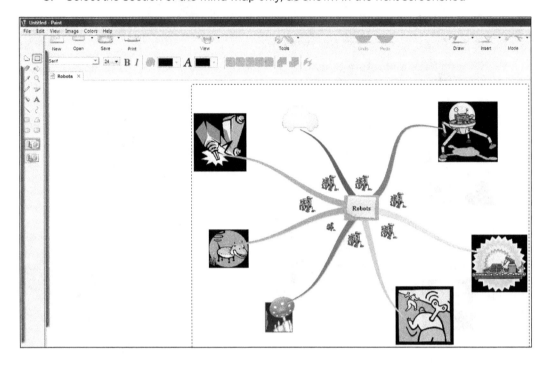

4. Save the image as `.png` so that you can upload the image of the mind map in the Moodle course.

Drawing pictures using pen sketch

It is also possible to use a digital pen, also known as pen sketch, to draw elements for the mind map. For example, as we are dealing with robots in this mind map, you can draw a robot's face and add it to the mind map, as shown in the next screenshot:

Creating a writing activity

You may add the mind map as a recourse in the Moodle course or you may insert an image in it. In both cases, students can write an article about robots. If you upload the mind map in the Moodle course, you can do it in the **Description** block of **Upload a single file** and you do not have to split the activity in two.

Adding data to pictures—creating a mind map using MindMeister

In this recipe, we are going to work with MindMeister software, which is free and open source. We are going to create a mind map, inserting links to websites, which contain information as well as pictures. Why? Because if we include more information in the mind map, we are going to lead our students on how to write. Apart from that, they are going to read more before writing and we are also exercising reading comprehension in a way. However, they may also summarize information if we create a link to a website. So let's get ready!

Getting ready

We are going to enter `http://www.mindmeister.com/` and then **Sign up for free**. There is one version which is free to use, or you may choose the other two that are commercial. After signing up, we are going to develop a mind map for our students to work with.

There is a video which is a tutorial explaining in a very simple and easy way on how to design a mind map using this software. So it is worth watching.

How to do it...

We are going to enter the previously mentioned website and we are going to start working on this new mind map. In this case, I have chosen the topic "Special days around the world". Follow these steps:

1. Click on **My New Mind Map** and write the name of the topic in the block in the middle.

2. Click on **Connect** and draw arrows, adding as many **New node** blocks as you wish.

3. Add a website giving information for each special occasion. Click on the Node, then click on **Extras–Links | Links** and complete the **URL** block, as shown in the next screenshot:

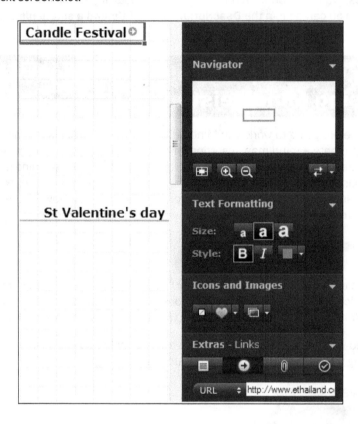

4. Then click on the checkmark icon. Repeat the same process for each occasion.
5. You can add icons or images to the nodes of the mind map.
6. Click on **Share Map** at the bottom of the page, as shown in the next screenshot:

7. Click on **Publish** and change the button to **ON**, as shown in the next screenshot:

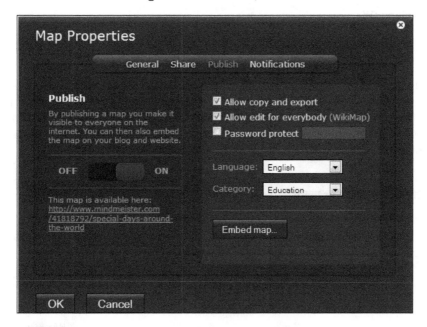

8. Select **Allow edit for everybody (WikiMap)**, as shown in the previous screenshot.

9. You can also embed the mind map. When you click on **Embed map**, the next screenshot will appear:

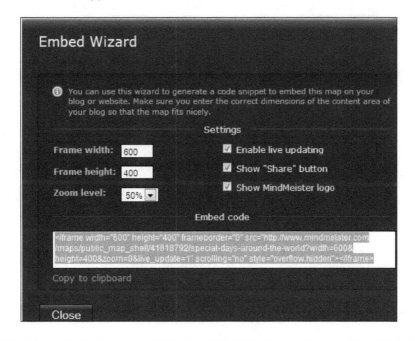

10. Copy the **Embed code** and click on **Close.**

11. Click on **OK**.

How it works...

After creating the mind map about special occasions around the world, we will either embed it or create a link to a website for our students to work on a writing activity. Here the proposal is to work through a Wiki because in **Map Properties** we have clicked on **Allow edit for everybody (WikiMap)** so that students can modify the mind map with their ideas. Select the Weekly outline section where you want to insert the activity and these are the steps you have to follow:

1. Click on **Add an activity** and select **Wiki**.

2. Complete the **Name** block.

3. Complete the **Summary** block. You may either embed the mind map or create a link to a website, as shown in the next screenshot:

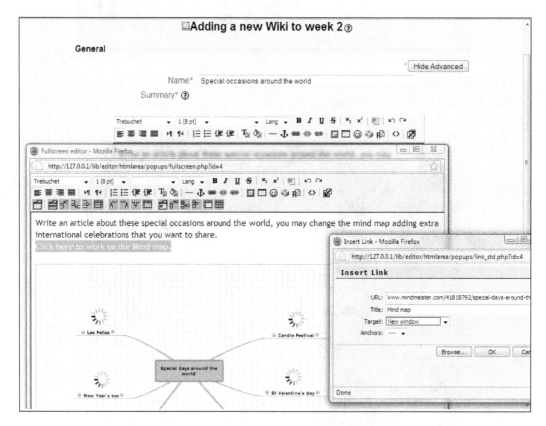

4. Click on **Save and return to course.**

Providing a situation to a story—drawing a mind map using Draw Anywhere

In this recipe, we are going to create a story using a mind map and we are going to add linking words or keywords so that our students follow those clues in order to carry out the writing activity. We are going to design the mind map using the `http://www.drawanywhere.com` website. Then we are going to save the mind map as an image and upload it in our Moodle course so that students will be able to see the mind map. So let's get ready!

Getting ready

We are going to enter the previously mentioned website and create an account. There are others accounts, which have more options, so you are free to choose. We are going to work with the free account. There is an interesting tutorial, which is worth watching, that explains how the software works, though it is very similar to the ones that we have been using.

How to do it...

After logging in, we are going to create a mind map. In this case, we are going to drag and drop the images on the left-hand side and we are going to draw a mind map with images. The difference from the first mind map is that in this case students have to write a story and we are going to include clues in the drawing in order to guide them with their writing. Linking words may be added as well. These are the steps that you have to follow:

1. Drag and drop images on the left-hand side to draw a "story mind map", as shown in the next screenshot:

2. Connect the pictures using the connectors from the menu.

3. Click on the image and then on the text icon in order to write some key and linking words.

4. Click on the mind map so that it fits in the screen of your computer and press the *Prt Scr* key.

5. Open Paint or any similar software and paste the image using *Ctrl + V*.

6. Click on **Select** and choose the mind map section. Click on **Edit** and select **Copy**.

7. Open a new file and paste the selected area of the mind map. Name the file with a .png extension. The mind map appears as shown in the next screenshot:

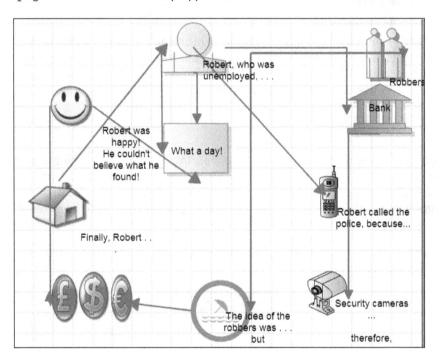

How it works...

It is time to upload the mind map in our Moodle course and create the activity. In this case, we are going to create the activity through an Assignment. So you are going to choose the Weekly outline section where you want to place the activity and follow these steps:

1. Click on **Add an activity** and select **Upload a single file** within Assignments.

2. Complete the **Assignment name** block.

3. Complete the **Description** block. Click on the **Insert image** icon and upload the mind map.

4. Click on **Save and return to course**.

5. The activity appears as shown in the next screenshot:

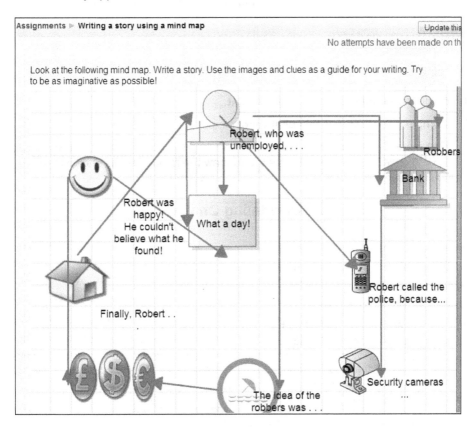

Creating mind maps using resources from Web 2.0

This is a very simple recipe. We are going to ask students to think about a topic and draw a mind map using resources from Web 2.0. In this way, they are going to practice the mind mapping technique so that they can organize their thoughts by themselves instead of being given clues. Later, as usual, they are going to write an article about that topic. So let's get ready to work!

Getting ready

We are going to carry out this activity in a Chat so that students can brainstorm among themselves, and we are going to create a link to a website where they can draw a mind map.

This is the first part of the activity, let's say the beginning of process writing. After they create the mind map, we are going to design the writing activity. We enter the course and select the Weekly outline section in which we want to add the activity. Let's Moodle it!

How to do it...

You are going to follow these steps in order to design the activity previously introduced:

1. Click on **Add an activity** and select **Chat**.

2. Complete the **Name of this chat room** block.

3. Complete the **Introduction text** block, inserting the link to `http://www.mindomo.com`, the website where students are to draw the mind map, as shown in the next screenshot:

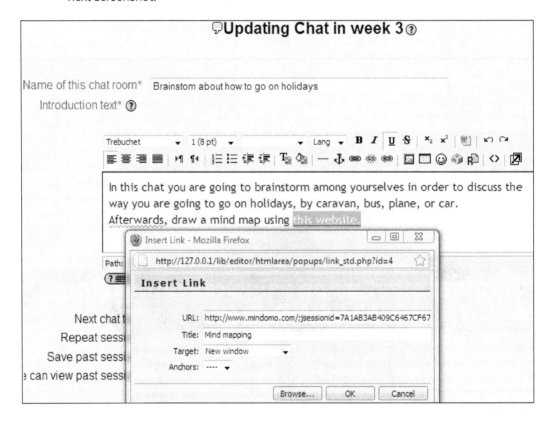

4. Complete the **Insert Link** block and click on **OK**.

5. Click on **Save and return to course**.

How it works...

After students brainstorm among themselves and draw the mind map, they have to carry out the writing activity. In this case, they are going to do it through **Advanced uploading of files** within Assignments (we are going to let them upload two files) because in that way they can upload both the mind map and the writing activity. These are the steps to follow:

1. Click on **Add an activity** and select **Advanced uploading of files** within Assignments.

2. Complete both the **Assignment name** and the **Description** blocks.

3. Click on **Save and return to course**.

Creating a tree diagram using Microsoft Word

A tree diagram is used to compare two different situations, topics, persons, or ideas in the same category. As opposed to a Venn diagram, in a tree diagram there are no similarities, so we are going to try to deal with two different topics to explore as many differences as possible. We can work with vocabulary, adjectives, and linking devices. A suitable piece of writing in this case would be an essay or article expressing the different views. As regards the drawing of the tree diagram, it may be either horizontal or vertical, so we are going to carry out both of them. Let's get ready to work!

Getting ready

We are going to draw a tree diagram about two different cultures and create two links to websites so that students can finish the diagrams. In this case, we are going to design them using Microsoft Word, but you are free to choose any other editor. In this recipe, we will be dealing with two countries whose customs are totally different—Egypt and Greenland.

How to do it...

You will be designing the tree diagram in Microsoft Word and comparing several aspects of both countries. The students are to complete the information provided by the websites from where they are to take the information. Therefore, in the following activity we are going to design a reading comprehension activity, a prewriting activity, and a writing one. Open Microsoft Word and follow these steps:

1. Click on **Insert** and choose **SmartArt**, then choose **Hierarchy**, and select **Horizontal Hierarchy**, as shown in the next screenshot:

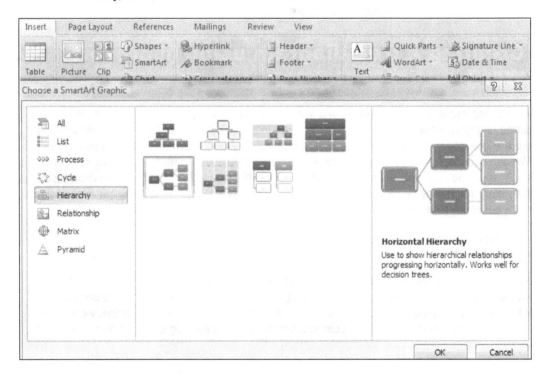

2. Insert two diagrams, one for Egypt and another one for Greenland, as shown in the following screenshot:

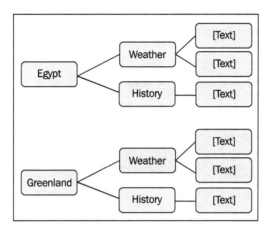

3. Save the file.

How it works...

We are going to create a writing activity in our Moodle course, so select the Weekly outline section where you want to place it. We will design it through an Essay within a Quiz, so these are the steps that you have to follow:

1. Click on **Add an activity** and select **Advanced uploading of files**.

2. Complete the **Assignment name** block.

3. Complete the **Description** block and create links to the two websites, one about Greenland and another one about Egypt.

4. Insert a link for the tree diagram file.

5. Click on **Save and return to course**.

6. The activity appears as shown in the next screenshot:

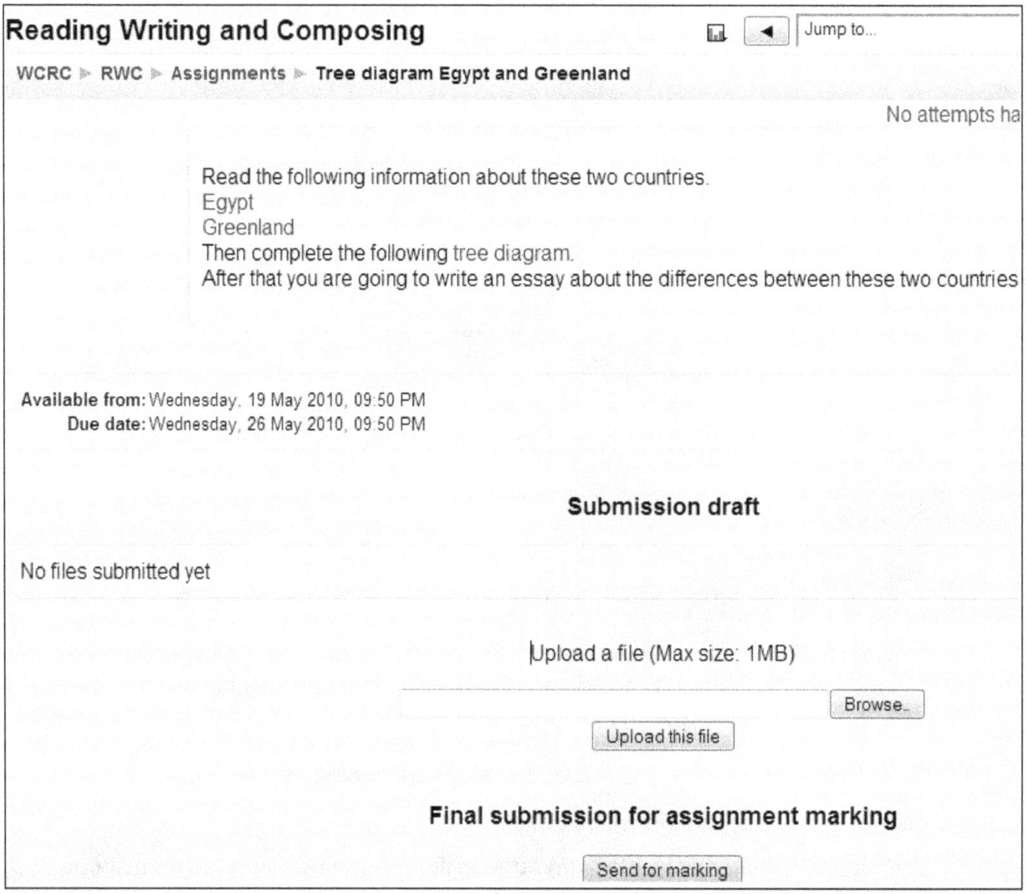

Reading Writing and Composing 🖬 ◀ | Jump to...

WCRC ▷ RWC ▷ Assignments ▷ **Tree diagram Egypt and Greenland**

No attempts ha

Read the following information about these two countries.
Egypt
Greenland
Then complete the following tree diagram.
After that you are going to write an essay about the differences between these two countries

Available from: Wednesday, 19 May 2010, 09:50 PM
Due date: Wednesday, 26 May 2010, 09:50 PM

Submission draft

No files submitted yet

Upload a file (Max size: 1MB)

| Browse...|

Upload this file

Final submission for assignment marking

Send for marking

Pictures in a tree diagram—creating a tree diagram using creately.com

We are going to create a tree diagram using images instead of words. Students are free to combine the pictures in their future writing, though we have to be very careful in choosing the right pictures. In this case, we are going to use the following website: http://creately.com, which is an excellent resource from our wonderful Web 2.0.

Getting ready

We are going to enter the website that we have mentioned before and we are going to sign in. Afterwards, we are going to choose a template to work with. In this case, we can select Decision Tree 1 or Blank Diagram to create it ourselves. Here I have decided to work with the first mentioned template.

How to do it...

These are the steps that you have to follow in order to create the tree diagram with images using the `http://creately.com` website:

1. Write a name for the document in the **Document Name** block.

2. Choose the template that you want to work with, as shown in the next screenshot:

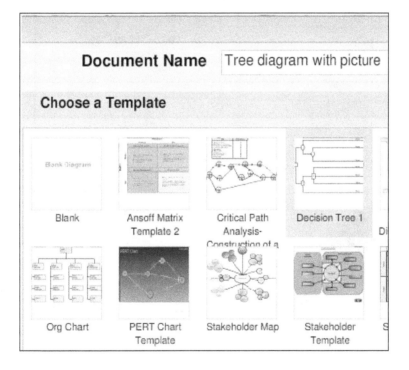

3. Click on **Create document**.

4. Drag and drop the images on the left-hand side and complete the diagram with pictures.

5. Save the diagram.

How it works...

After virtually drawing the diagram, we are going to get into our Moodle course and choose the Weekly outline section where we want to place the activity. In this case, we are going to create a Forum activity in which students can choose a title for this story, that is to say they are going to brainstorm using this diagram. These are the steps that you have to follow:

1. Click on **Add an activity** and select **Forum**.

2. Complete the **Forum name** and **Forum introduction**.

3. Go back to the website of the tree diagram and click on **Embed image**, as shown in the next screenshot:

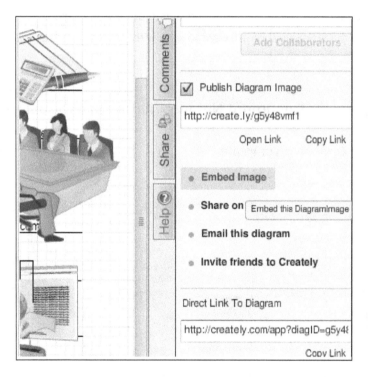

4. Click on **Select and Copy**, as shown in the next screenshot:

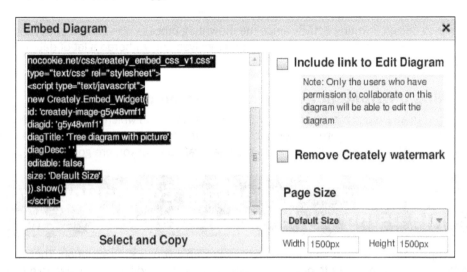

5. Go back to the Moodle course and click on the **Toggle HTML Source** icon and paste the embedding code. Then click on the same icon again.

6. Click on **Save and return to course**.

7. The activity appears as shown in the next screenshot:

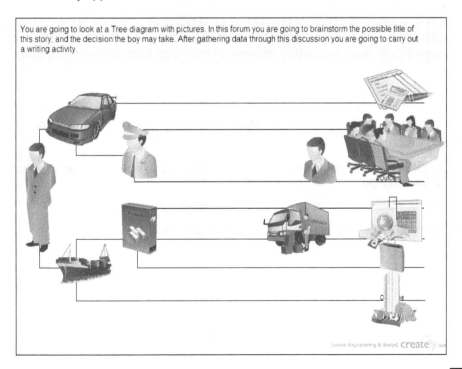

There's more...

You can also design a writing activity since the prewriting process was carried out by the Forum activity. Students brainstormed among themselves and gathered a lot of data in order to write a story.

Designing a writing activity out of the tree diagram

You can create an Upload a single file activity or an Offline one in which students write what they have discussed in the Forum. They may have written the story while discussing, but that is the first part of the process of writing. So the final draft is what you are going to design here.

Completing a tree diagram comparing two people using my.lovelycharts.com

In this simple recipe our students are going to work with a very simple situation. They are going to compare themselves to one of their classmates. It would be a good idea to create a chat activity if some students add some comments on differences between these people. Let's get ready.

Getting ready

We are going to enter the `http://www.lovelycharts.com/`, website and we are going to sign in. Afterwards we are going to login and start working. In this website, we cannot choose a template with a decision tree or tree diagram, so we are going to create it using arrows.

How to do it...

After entering the website mentioned previously, we are going to create a tree diagram. Follow these steps:

1. Click on **Basic symbols** on the left-hand side and drag and drop them in order to form a tree diagram.

2. Double-click on them in order to write text inside the symbols.

3. Click on **File** and select **Save** in order to save the diagram.

4. Click on **File** and select **Export** and the following screenshot will appear:

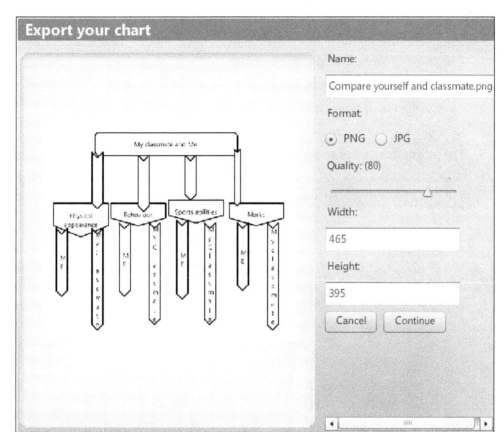

5. Click on **Continue**.
6. Save the file.

How it works...

We are going to create the activity in our Moodle course. In this case, we are going to create a Chat activity so that other classmates can describe differences that the classmates may not realize, due to the fact that third parties see things from a different point of view.

Select the Weekly outline section where you want to place the activity and these are the steps that you have to follow:

1. Click on **Add an activity** and select **Chat**.

2. Complete the **Name of this chat room** block.

3. Complete the **Introduction text** block.

4. Click on the **Insert image** icon, search for the image, and then upload it.

5. Click on **Save and return to course**.

6. The activity appears as shown in the next screenshot:

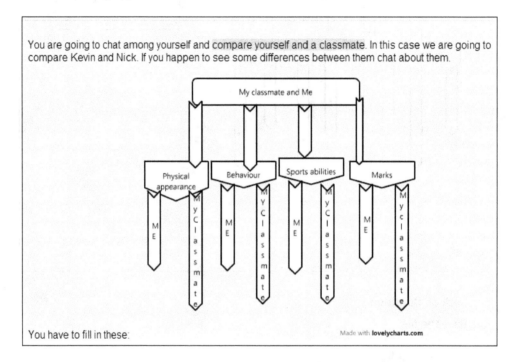

You are going to chat among yourself and compare yourself and a classmate. In this case we are going to compare Kevin and Nick. If you happen to see some differences between them chat about them.

You have to fill in these:

Made with **lovelycharts.com**

We can take advantage of the brainstorming work that students carry out through the chat activity, and we can create a writing activity. They have already gathered data about this topic in order to complete the prewriting step.

Creating a description activity out of the tree diagram

You can design a Journal or an **Offline activity** in which students can write the personal description of two students specifying the differences between them that they found out in the chat room. Some linking devices expressing contrast can be included in the title or the activity.

Comparing the Flintstones and the Simpsons—using cacoo.com to create a tree diagram

Which are the most famous cartoon families on TV? Yes, the title of the recipe has already answered this question! The Simpsons and the Flintstones—though they may have some similarities, in this case we are only going to focus on the differences. We are going to create a tree diagram to compare both of them, although not all students may know about the Flintstones. We may create a tree diagram with images to highlight the differences.

Getting ready

We are going to carry out this recipe using `http://cacoo.com/`, which is a website where you can create different types of diagrams, flowcharts, and mind maps. In this case, we are going to create a tree diagram focusing on the differences of these two great families. After that, students are going to write an article about them gathering the data used in this tree diagram.

How to do it...

First of all, you have to enter the previously mentioned website and follow the process that you carried out with the previous activities. You have to sign up and after that sign in. Then you can watch the tutorial on how to use the website, which is quite interesting. Then create the tree diagram by following these steps:

1. Click on **Create New Diagram**.

2. Draw the diagram and drag and drop the elements you need in order to create it, as shown in the next screenshot:

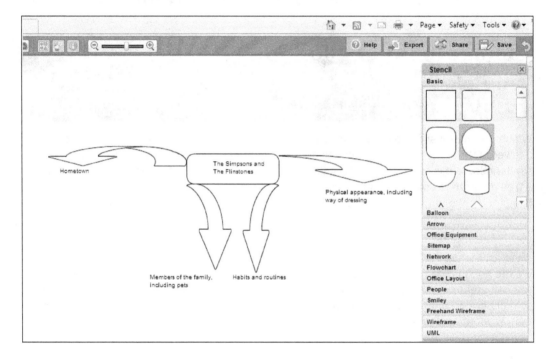

3. Click on **Save** and complete the fields, as shown in the next screenshot:

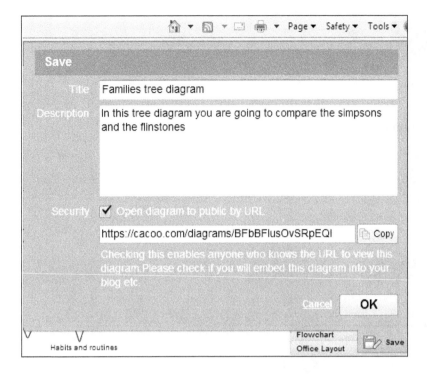

4. You may check the Security box in order to **Open diagram to public by URL**, as shown in the previous screenshot. Then click on **OK**.

5. After we click on OK the Save drop-down closes. You then click on the arrow on the top right hand margin next to the **Save** icon.

6. Click on the **Link** icon and copy the embed code, as shown in the next screenshot:

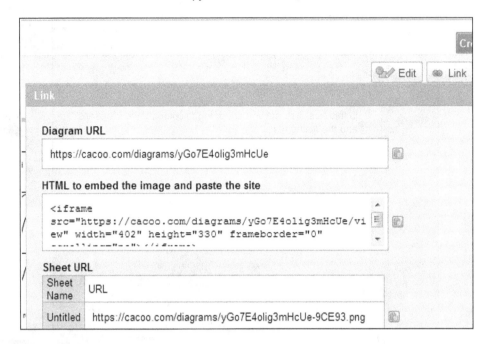

How it works...

The first part of the activity is ready, that is to say the prewriting part. Now it is time to design the writing activity. Therefore, we will create the activity in our Moodle course and the students can complete the tree diagram in `http://cacoo.com/`. Afterwards, they will perform the writing activity using the data from the tree diagram. Choose the Weekly outline section where you want to add the activity and follow these steps:

1. Click on **Add an activity** and select **Offline activity** within Assignments.

2. Complete the **Assignment name** block.

3. Complete the **Description** block.

4. Click on the **Toggle HTML Source** icon and paste the embed code.

5. Click on **Save and return to course**. The activity appears as shown in the following screenshot:

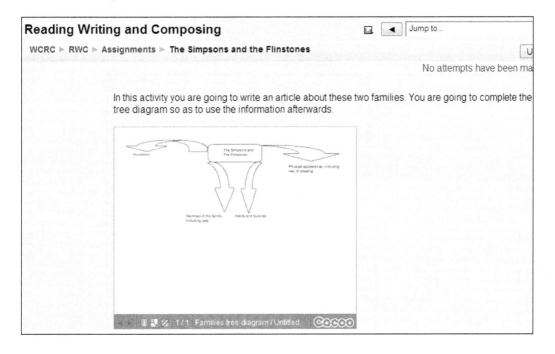

10
Preparing a Discussion Clock

When preparing a discussion clock, we have to bear in mind that students should explore twelve different aspects of a situation, topic, and so on. In some cases, it is not possible, so we are going to think of different ways of preparing such a discussion clock so that students can take advantage of it. The result of this technique is wonderful because the pieces of writing are longer, therefore students may write either articles or essays, as well as pieces of writing concerning engineering.

This is the main reason why this is the last chapter of the book. Besides, it is the widest technique covered in this cookbook to cover a topic. We are going to design different types of discussion clocks in order to work with several types of intelligences as well as ways of relating items.

In this chapter, we will cover the following topics:

- How to prepare a discussion clock—words to cover different viewpoints
- Writing from a viewpoint—using tiny URLs in the discussion clock
- Picturing the clock diagram—adding images
- Music in the clock diagram—embedding MP3 files to our Moodle course
- Just words—using a target diagram to create a discussion clock and creating a story out of it
- Questions in the clock diagram—writing a newspaper article
- Correcting through a clock diagram
- Designing a discussion clock in order to create an aircraft using resources from Web 2.0

Introduction

In this chapter, you will be able to design a writing technique in which students will be able to explore a topic from other points of view. Thus, they will not be trapped in only one viewpoint. This discussion clock does not have two hands but twelve, because each one (which belongs to each number) is going to focus on a different topic.

It is very wise to move away to another point of view, so in that way we can consider many aspects and alternatives. The finding of new options is the desired outcome. Those elements are a 'must' in using the thinking skill properly. Therefore, the discussion clock is the technique to work with when we want to encourage our students to plan their writing in this way.

We are going to draw several types of discussion clocks to be creative ourselves as well. Some students can be much more productive with some variants of clocks than others, due to the fact that their thinking is better when working with images, music, questions, words, and so on.

The last recipe of this chapter is a very interesting one, due to the fact that we are going to design an aircraft using resources from Web 2.0. With this website, we can design different types of aircraft in 3D. Besides, they will increase their vocabulary in the engineering field, and write technical pieces of writing, which they haven't up to now.

How to prepare a discussion clock—words to cover different viewpoints

In this task, we are going to prepare a basic discussion clock. We are going to choose a topic and we are going to draw a clock using Microsoft Word. In each of the numbers of the clock, we are going to draw an arrow and at the point of the arrow we are going to write a word. That word is going to be the angle to be explored for the main topic.

Getting ready

First of all, we are going to choose a topic to explore—for example 'Television'. Afterwards, we are going to choose twelve aspects to explore this topic, because we are going to write those twelve words next to the numbers of the clock.

How to do it...

Enter Microsoft Word and insert an image of a clock, try to choose an attractive one. Then you are going to write the words, and the viewpoints that you want your students to explore. Follow these steps to create the discussion clock:

1. Click on **Insert**, and select **Clip Art**.

2. Look for a clock and insert it.

3. Click on **Format | Text Wrapping | Through** as shown in the next screenshot:

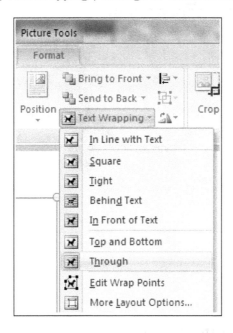

4. Click on **Insert** and select **Shapes**, then click on **Arrow**, as shown in the next screenshot:

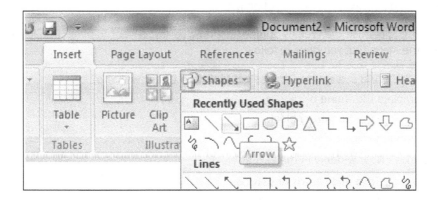

5. Draw twelve lines, one for each number and write twelve words related to **TELEVISION** that students have to explore, as shown in the next screenshot:

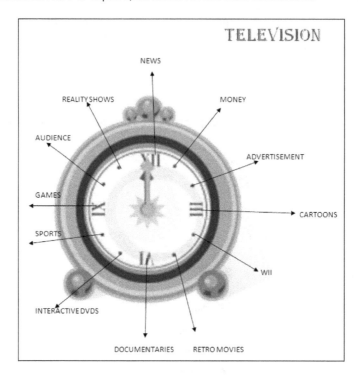

6. Save the file.

How it works...

We have just finished drawing the discussion clock, so we have to upload it to our Moodle course. Therefore, we are going to create a link to a file and afterwards we are going to create an activity in which students have to upload a file. The first activity is the prewriting activity and the second activity is the writing of an article.

You are going to choose the Weekly outline section where you want to place the activity and these are the steps that you have to follow:

1. Click on **Add a resource**, and select **Link to a file or website**.
2. Complete the **Name** block.
3. Complete the **Summary** block.
4. Upload the file.
5. Choose **New window** in the **Target** block.
6. Click on **Save and return to course**.

There's more...

We have already created the first part of the activity, therefore we have to design the writing section.

Creating a writing activity

After creating a link to the file, we are going to design the writing activity. Students are going to upload the file in which they are going to write an article about television taking into account the twelve topics that they have covered in the discussion clock.

Writing from a viewpoint—using tiny URLs in the discussion clock

In this recipe, we are going to work with a divided discussion clock. That is to say that each student is going to give their viewpoint about a certain topic to be covered. For example, in this case we are going to work with 'Earthquakes'. There are several aspects to be covered in this topic, thus we can make several links to websites, if possible twelve, statistics would support the idea that not all our students will click on the same website. According to the website that they read they are going to express their viewpoint on different topics and also give their own ideas.

Getting ready

We do have to surf the Web and find twelve links to websites which deal with earthquakes. So, this is the first thing to do! Afterwards, we are going to create the discussion clock in a Microsoft Word document or in any other similar software and we are going to shorten the URLs before copying them in the discussion clock.

When the discussion clock has been designed, we are going to carry out the activity in a Wiki so that students can write collaboratively. Afterwards, each student is going to design his or her own final draft gathering the data that each of them had written in an **Online text** activity.

This activity is like the old fashioned way of writing, that you had to write one sentence and pass the piece of paper either backwards or forwards. Though, in this case we are guiding the writing, and doing a reading comprehension activity before the act of writing.

How to do it...

We are going to design the discussion clock in Microsoft Word, as I have already mentioned, and shorten the URL of the websites that we have chosen. In order to shorten the URLs, you can enter the following website and follow these steps:

1. Enter the following website: `http://www.tiny.cc/`.
2. Copy and paste the URL in the block, as shown in the next screenshot:

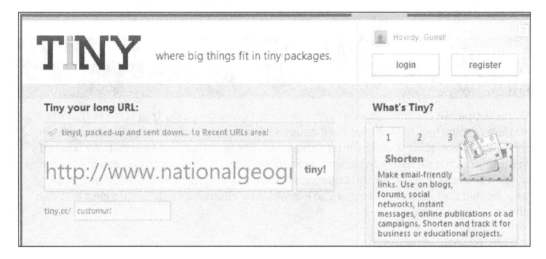

3. Click on **tiny!**.
4. Copy the shortened address and paste it in the discussion clock that you have designed in Microsoft Word, as shown in the next screenshot:

5. Repeat the same process twelve times!

6. Save the file.

Enter the Moodle course and select the Weekly outline section where you want to add the activity. Add a resource and create a link to this file.

How it works...

We are going to enter into the Moodle course and select the Weekly outline section where we want to design the activity. Remember that the first part of the activity is the Wiki, so these are the steps that you have to follow:

1. Click on **Add an activity** and select **Wiki**.

2. Complete the **Name** block.

3. Complete the **Summary** block.

4. Click on **Save and return to course**.

There's more...

We have already created one writing activity, and we have to design another type of writing activity.

Creating another writing activity

You can create another writing activity in which students gather the data from their classmates and write their own articles taking into account all the aspects. It would be like a great summary of all the websites. We are lucky if they have explored them all. So, an **Online text** would be a good idea.

Picturing the clock diagram—adding images

In this recipe, we are going to work with another variation of a clock diagram. We are going to design it using Microsoft Visio. We are going to do it using a pie chart and add images to it. In this case, we are going to explore the topic concerning a very brave profession 'The life of a fire fighter'. This topic can lead to a great piece of writing due to the fact that many things can be suggested for this topic.

Getting ready

We are going to enter Microsoft Visio or any similar software in order to create a pie chart divided in twelve pieces, simulating a clock with twelve different viewpoints. Next, to each piece of the pie we are going to insert a picture, which would lead to a different viewpoint of the fire fighter's job.

Then we are going to upload the file to our Moodle course and we are going to create a writing activity using a Journal.

How to do it...

We are going to enter Microsoft Visio, or any similar software. Then you are going to follow these steps in order to create the previously mentioned discussion clock:

1. Click on **Business** in the **Template category**, and select **Charts and Graphs**, as shown in the next screenshot:

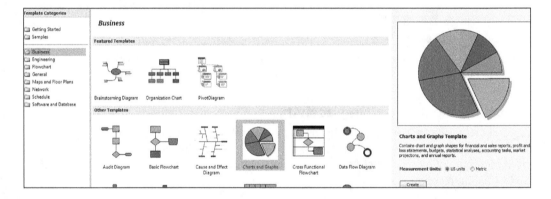

2. Click on **Pie chart** and drag and drop it to the sheet, as shown in the next screenshot:

3. Click on **Define** in the block that appears. Add **11** and **12** in the **Format** block.

4. Write **12** in the **Value** block, as shown in the next screenshot:

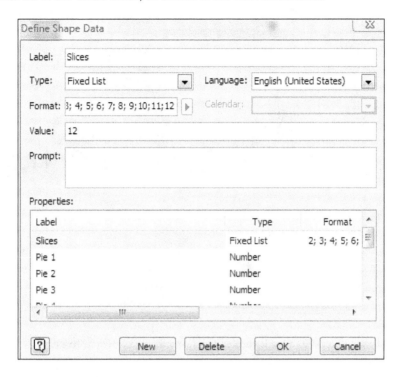

5. Click on **OK** twice, because two blocks will appear.

6. Click on **Insert** and select **Picture**, and then select **Clipart**.

7. Add pictures to the diagram, as shown in the next screenshot:

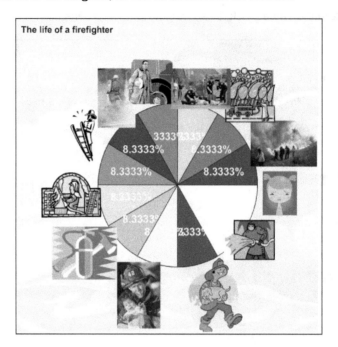

8. Save the file as **JPEG File Interchange Format**, as shown in the next screenshot:

How it works...

We are going to upload this discussion clock to our Moodle course. We are going to select the Weekly outline section where we want to design the activity. We are going to design the activity in a Journal, you may also design it in **Upload a single file**, so these are the steps that you have to follow:

1. Click on **Add an activity** and select **Journal**.

2. Complete both the **Journal name** and **question**.

3. Click on the **Insert Image** icon and upload the image of the discussion clock.

4. Click on **Save and return to course**.

5. The activity appears as shown in the next screenshot:

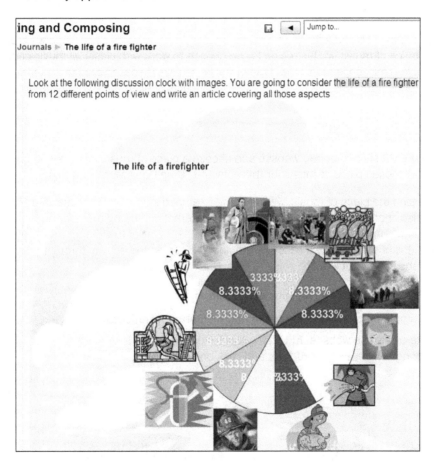

Music in the clock diagram—embedding MP3 files to our Moodle course

In this recipe, we are going to work on the theory of bilateral thinking, that is to say that both hemispheres of the brain work together. The right side of the brain will put bits of information together to make an entire picture of the piece of music that they are listening to; while the left side of the brain will understand the language (writing).

In order to illustrate this theory, we are going to work with a diagram clock using music. Out of a piece of music, students are going to think of twelve aspects to explore and they are going to carry out a writing activity afterwards.

Getting ready

We are going to enter the following website: `http://www.archive.org` and we are going to choose a piece of music. In this recipe I have chosen to work with classical music concerning Christmas. You may chose any other type of music you like, because students may find it easier to connect the piece of music to different aspects concerning a well known holiday.

How to do it...

Enter the previously mentioned website and choose a piece of music to embed in our Moodle course. The chosen piece of music for this activity is 'Ding Dong Merrily on High'.

After choosing the piece of music, we are going to embed said piece of music in a Forum or you may also choose a chat activity. Through this interaction among themselves they are going to establish which twelve aspects they have to consider in order to write an article based on the said piece of music. In this case, we are going to design the activity through a Forum, so these are the steps that you are going to follow:

1. Click on **Add an activity**, and select **Forum**.

2. Complete both the **Forum name** and the **Forum introduction** block.

3. Return to the website, `http://www.archive.org/details/DingDongMerrilyOnHigh`, and click on **embed this**, as shown in the next screenshot:

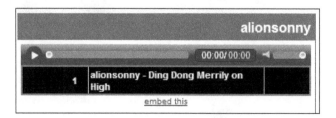

4. Click on play, as indicated in the following pop out window, as shown in the next screenshot:

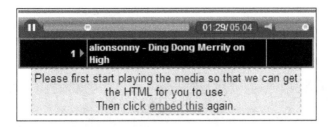

5. Click on **embed this** and copy the embedding code.

6. Go back to the Moodle course. Click on the **Toggle HTML Source** icon and paste the embedding code.

7. Click on the **Toggle HTML Source** icon again, the following will appear, as shown in the next screenshot:

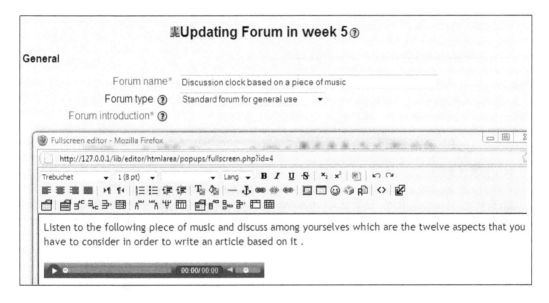

8. Click on **Save and return to course**.

How it works...

Students are going to listen to the music and interact among themselves in the Forum activity. Later, they are going to choose which are the twelve aspects to bear in mind in order to write an article out of this piece of music, so one option is to design an **Online text** activity for them to write.

Just words—using a target diagram to create a discussion clock and creating a story out of it

This is a very interactive recipe. Why? The answer is very simple. We are going to embed the target diagram available from the `http://classtools.net` website, which is very similar to the clock diagram, because it is divided into 12 parts in the outer layer. Just words are going to be enough for the process writing in this task.

We are going to embed the target diagram in a Forum activity so that students can interact among themselves and discuss which are the words to be incorporated in the outer layer. Thus, they are going to brainstorm before writing the story.

The story is to be created using the following website: `http://myths.e2bn.org/story_creator/`, which is a fantastic website to work with. It would be great to work with myths, legends, or epic stories because of the characters provided.

Getting ready

We have to enter the first website mentioned in order to start designing our discussion clock, which is to be a target diagram in this case. We have to give a clear idea to our students which is the topic of the story to be written, so that they can work on the brainstorming through a Forum activity.

How to do it...

Enter `http://classtools.net` and follow these steps in order to create the discussion clock in this recipe:

1. Click on **Target**, as shown in the next screenshot:

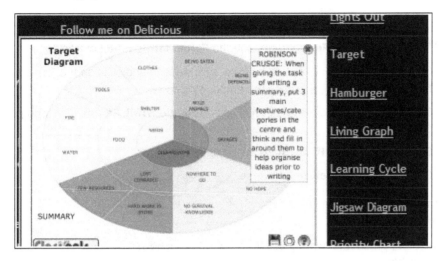

2. We are going to complete the **Name** block, as well as the **Notes/Instructions** block.

3. Complete the centre of the diagram, as shown in the following screenshot:

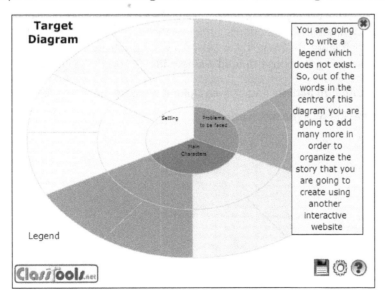

4. Click on the **Save as Web Page** icon, in order to save the file.

How it works...

We are going to embed the **Target Diagram** into our Moodle course. Therefore, we can design the Forum activity in which students are to discuss which other words would be useful to insert in it. Choose the Weekly outline section where you want to insert the activity. These are the steps to follow:

1. Click on **Add an activity** and select **Forum**.

2. Complete both the **Forum name** and the **Forum introduction** blocks.

3. Go back to the `http://classtools.net` website and click on the **Embed into blog/webpage** icon, and copy the embedding code.

4. Go back to the Moodle course and click on **Toggle HTML Source** icon, and paste the embedding code.

5. Click on the **Toggle HTML Source** icon again.

6. Click on **Save and return to course**.

There's more...

We can also design another writing activity after students have brainstormed among themselves.

Designing a creating a story activity through Web 2.0

We are going to design a story writing activity using the target diagram or discussion clock used in the Forum activity. After students complete the diagram with the words that they are going to use in their story, we are going to design a writing activity in the Moodle course. In this recipe, we are going to choose **Upload a single file**. Follow these steps:

1. Click on **Add an activity** and choose **Upload a single file** within Assignments.

2. Complete the **Assignment name** block.

3. Complete the **Description** block and create a link to the following website: `http://myths.e2bn.org/story_creator/`, as shown in the next screenshot:

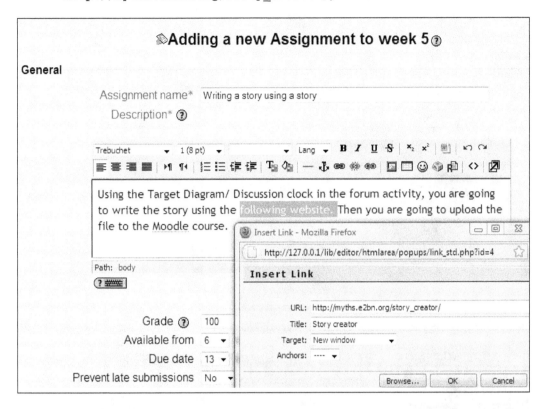

4. Complete the **Insert Link** block, as shown in the previous screenshot.

5. Click on **Save and return to course**.

6. When students click on the link to the website they can create a situation and write the story beneath the drawing, a sample is shown in the next screenshot:

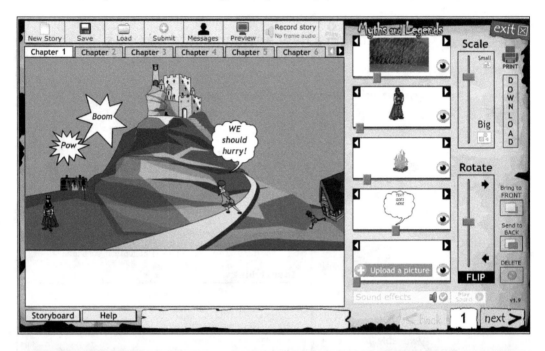

Questions in the clock diagram—writing a newspaper article

Questions are used many times in reading comprehension activities as well as in prewriting ones. When they are answered accurately and by adding all the necessary information, they may become a key part of the future piece of writing to be carried out by our students. Therefore, we could not leave aside the opportunity to cope with this in the discussion clock. So let's work with this technique of inserting questions in the clock. In this recipe, we are going to ask students to write a newspaper article and we are going to lead their writing with questions.

Getting ready

We are going to design a glossary in which students are going to write the definitions of all the words indicating the different parts of the newspaper article, so as to bear them in mind when writing it. Apart from that, they have to consider different fonts as well as font size as similar as possible to the real ones in order to do it .

How to do it...

You are going to choose the Weekly outline section in which you want to place the activity. Then, follow these steps:

1. Click on **Add an activity**, and select **Glossary**.

2. Complete the **Name** block.

3. Complete the **Description** block, writing all the words that you want your students to look for, they may also add others relevant to this topic.

4. You can also create a link to an online dictionary, for example: `http://dictionary.cambridge.org/`.

5. Click on **Save and return to course**.

6. The activity appears as shown in the next screenshot:

How it works...

We are going to design the discussion clock with questions after students have investigated the different parts of a newspaper article. Apart from that they may not be used to reading one. We are going to design this activity in **Offline activity**, so these are the steps that you have to follow:

1. Click on **Add an activity** and select **Offline activity** within Assignments.

2. Complete both the **Assignment name** and the **Description** block, as shown in the following screenshot:

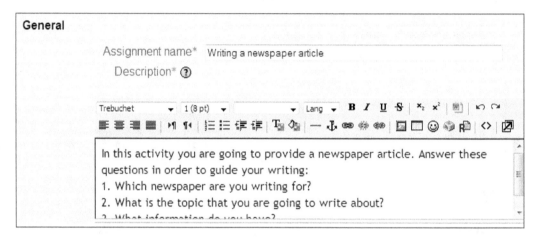

3. Click on **Save and return to course**.

4. The activity is ready for your students to write!

There's more...

We can also design the writing activity simulating the template of a newspaper.

Creating a writing activity using the template of a newspaper

We can write the question of the activity in the template of a newspaper. It is a very appealing way to work on it due to the fact that images attract the attention to students. We are going to work with the following website: `http://www.fodey.com/generators/newspaper/snippet.asp`. Thus, these are the steps that you have to follow:

1. Complete the blank blocks with the information that you want to give to your students, as shown in the next screenshot:

Name of the newspaper:

Moodle News

Date:

Wednesday, March, 2010

Headline:

Write a newspaper article

Enter your story:

```
In this activity you are going to provide a newspaper
article. Answer the following 12 questions in order to
explore different aspects and guide your writing:
1. Which newspaper are you writing for?
2. What is the topic that you are going to write about?
3. What information do you have?
```

Please do **not** use the names of
real newspapers or persons.

Generate!

2. Click on **Generate** and the newspaper template will have your data, as shown in the next screenshot:

3. Click on **Download your Image** and click on **Save**.

4. Click on **Save** again.

5. Go to the Moodle course and select the Weekly outline section where you want to place the activity. Follow the previous steps to set up the **Offline activity**.

6. In the **Description** block, click on the **Insert picture** icon, and upload the image.

7. Click on **Save and return to course**, the activity appears as shown in the next screenshot:

Correcting through a clock diagram

In this recipe, we are going to work on reviewing a file from Microsoft Word and correcting a piece of writing which was submitted by our students. Therefore, we are going to switch our role to teacher, in order to correct the file, as shown in the next screenshot:

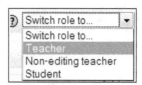

Getting ready

We are going to open the file in a Microsoft Word document and we are going to correct it using the **Review** offered by this software. Thus, we have to click on the activity that we want to correct and open the file.

How to do it...

After opening the file in Microsoft Word we are going to follow these steps to work on the correcting process, in order to give some feedback to our students.

1. Click on **Review** and click on **Track Changes**, as shown in the next screenshot:

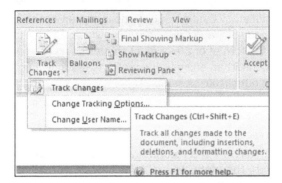

2. Click again on **Track changes**, as shown in the previous screenshot.

3. Click on **New Comment**, as shown in the next screenshot:

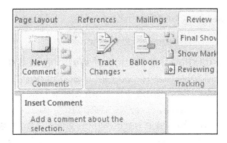

4. You are going to insert the comments as if you were correcting the paper with a pen, as shown in the next screenshot:

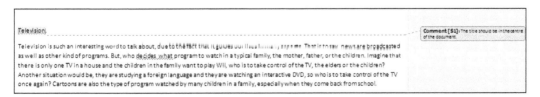

How it works...

After correcting your students' files, you are going to upload them to the Moodle course so that they can work on their mistakes and hand in the second draft afterwards.

Designing a discussion clock in order to create an aircraft using resources from Web 2.0

This is a very interesting recipe concerning aviation. We are going to create our own aircraft and explore 12 viewpoints before achieving the final result. We are going to use a free and open source website modified by Cristian Cuba, who is an aerospace engineer, and proficient in the previously mentioned field, and Carlos Varrenti, who is soon to be an aerospace engineer. They changed the format of the original shapes so as to assemble different types of aircrafts. We are going to insert an engineering profile to teach writing, because there may be some future engineers in our virtual classroom!

Getting ready

We are going to design an aircraft and students will have to design the clock diagram that they are going to work with. Therefore, we are going to work with **Advanced uploading of files** within Assignments in our Moodle course.

How to do it...

We are going to enter the following website: http://airplaneassembly.webs.com/. Then we are going to **Register** in order to use the website, which is free and open source.

We can also make our students read the section of **Working in 3 dimensions** which may be very interesting for our students, due to the fact that it is not the same as working in two dimensions, thus in our Moodle course we can make a link to this part of the website: http://airplaneassembly.webs.com/WEBPROTECT-workingin3dimensions. htm. Besides, they can also read Airplane parts which gives a brief as well as an interesting explanation of the different parts of the plane: http://airplaneassembly.webs.com/ airplaneparts.htm.

After reading **Working in 3 Dimensions**, you can read **How to use the Program**, which gives a detailed explanation of how to work with the software. Later, you are going to sign in in order to use the website and follow these steps:

1. Click on **Downloads**, so as to download the software, as shown in the next screenshot:

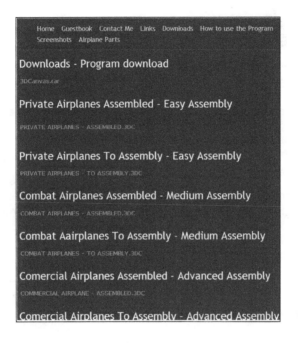

2. Click on the type of aircraft that you want to design, as shown in the previous screenshot.

3. If you choose **Private Airplanes To Assembly.3DC**, you are going to assemble the aircraft just by dragging and dropping the pieces, as shown in the next screenshot:

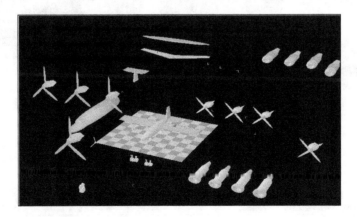

4. In the image there appear three different colors which indicate the axis that we are working with, either X, Y, or Z.

5. Click on **File** and select **Save as**, in order to save the image.

6. Click on **Start | All programs | Snipping Tool** in order to capture the image and save it as `.png` in order to upload it to our Moodle course.

How it works...

After choosing the Weekly outline section in which you want to display the activity, you are going to follow these steps:

1. Click on **Add an activity**, and select **Advanced Uploading of files** within Assignment.

2. Complete the **Assignment name** block.

3. Complete the **Description** block, and create a link to the previously mentioned websites.

4. Click on the **Insert Image** icon in order to upload the picture of the aircraft already designed.

5. Click on **Save and return to course**.

6. The activity is as shown in the next screenshot:

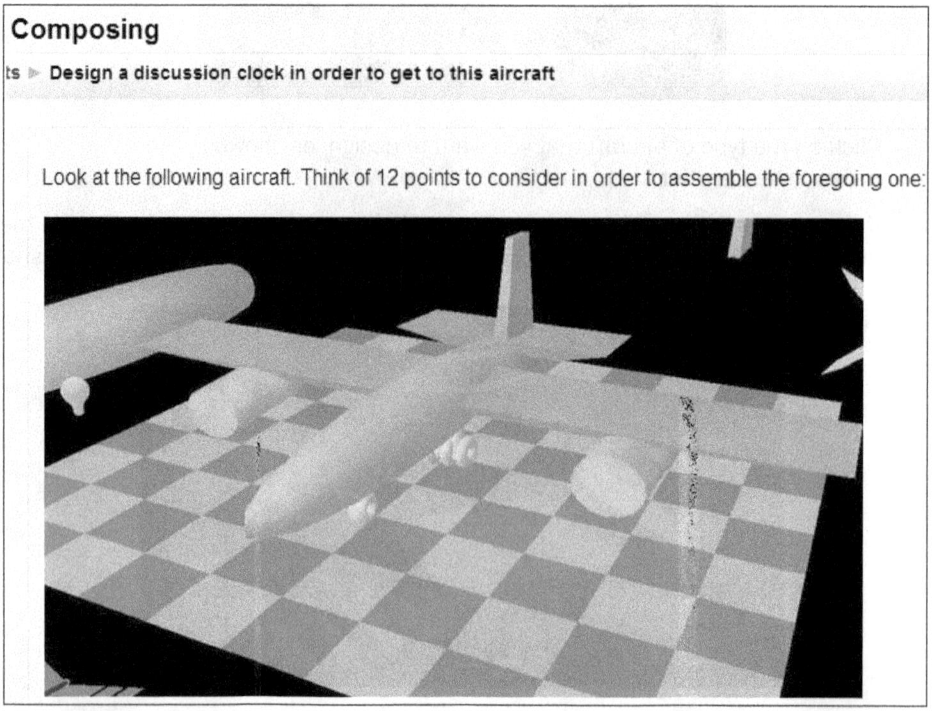

Composing

ts ▷ **Design a discussion clock in order to get to this aircraft**

Look at the following aircraft. Think of 12 points to consider in order to assemble the foregoing one:

There's more...

We can also design another type of writing activity using Facebook, since the previously mentioned website has a public group in this social network.

Using Facebook to create another writing activity

The website has a link to Facebook, so we can add a Facebook button as we have done in *Chapter 5, Creating stories using Twitter and Facebook* and students can join the group in order to discuss the creation of an airplane or the designing of the discussion clock. That is to say, which aspects they have to consider when designing the aircraft. The Facebook account is shown in the next screenshot:

Index

Venn diagram, drawing 190-192

Edraw Software
URL 122

endangered animals recipe
example 33, 34

essay correcting activity 166, 167

exercise activity
creating 47

F

Facebook
chain composition activity, designing 140
fishbone diagram, designing 122, 123
group activity, designing 137, 139
story writing activity, designing 136
survey exercise, creating in Moodle 15-18
URL 17, 124
writing activity, creating 279

Facebook button
inserting, into Moodle course 126, 127
URL 126

fairy tale updating recipe
about 196
journal activity, creating 198
writing activity, database used 197

Family Educational Rights and Privacy Act.
See **FERPA**

FERPA
about 19
URL 19

flowchart
designing, in OpenOffice 50

Forum
choices, justifying by students 39

Forum activity
creating 39, 51, 75
designing 20
working 21

G

game
designing 94, 98, 99
embedding 102
inserting, into Moodle 100
playing 100

game embedding recipe
journal activity, creating 102

glossary activity
creating 72
creating, with characters 72
crossword, creating 72

H

hamburger paragraph recipe
about 112
designing 113
journal activity, creating 114
paragraph writing, burger diagram used 114

Hot Potatoes
about 6
biography, unjumbling 13
comprehension activity, creating 14
comprehension activity, link adding 14
comprehension activity, working 15
crossword, creating 72, 73
downloading 10
matching activity, creating 12
matching activity, JMatch used 10
URL 10

Hot Potatoes quiz
accessing, steps 11
showing, in Moodle 10

Hot Potatoes quiz activity
creating 73

HTML block, Moodle course
Twitter button, inserting 121

I

images
adding, to clock diagram 259-262

information summarizing recipe
about 142
journal activity, creating 143

iPad
Alice in Wonderland, reading 84

iPhone
Alice in Wonderland, reading 84

iPod touch
Alice in Wonderland, reading 84

Ishikawa diagram
URL 121

J

journal activity
  creating 27-34, 45, 57-61, 71, 76, 92

K

Kaoru Ishikawa 121
KiwiTech 84

L

lesson activity
  creating 22-25
  quiz, answering 22-24
link
  creating, with Microsoft file 32, 33
lovelycharts
  URL 244

M

matching activity
  creating 6, 7
  creating, in Hot Potatoes 12
  designing 9
  designing, in Hot Potatoes 10
  designing, in OpenOffice 50
Microsoft file
  link, creating 32, 33
Microsoft Visio
  clock diagram, designing 259
Microsoft Visio 2007
  URL 185
  Venn diagram, drawing 185-188
Microsoft Word
  comic strip, creating 40, 41
  discussion clock, creating 254-256
  drawings, uploading from 29-31
  pictures, uploading from 25-29
  tree diagram, creating 237, 239
  Venn diagram, drawing with clip art 173-175
mind map
  about 221
  creating, MindMeister used 229-232
  creating, Web 2.0 resources used 235, 237
  drawing, Draw Anywhere used 233, 234
  images, inserting 223

  uploading, as .png file 227
MindMeister
  mind map, creating 229-232
  URL 229
Mindomo
  URL 236
MoMA 53
Moodle 1.9.5
  about 5
  advising campaigns, designing 58-60
  biography writing, link used 24, 25
  book, selecting by cover 57, 58
  compound sentences exercise, creating 6
  comprehension activity, creating 13
  comprehension, picturing 36-39
  cooking recipes, writing 60, 61
  drawings, uploading from Microsoft Word
      29-31
  endangered animals, writing about 33, 34
  Hot Potatoes quiz, showing 10
  images connecting, Forums used 19-21
  link, creating with Microsoft file 32, 33
  matching activity, adding 6, 7
  matching activity, designing 9
  paintings, working with 53-56
  paragraph, matching with picture 45-49
  pictures, uploading from Microsoft Word
      25-29
  quiz, answering 22-24
  sentences, connecting 13
  sentences, matching 6-9
  sentences, unjumbling 13
  stories, matching with flowchart 49-53
  survey exercise creating, Facebook used
      15-18
  survey exercise creating, Twitter used 15-18
  text, matching to speech bubbles 40-44
  websites, linking to 33, 34
Moodle course
  adventure, changing 80, 82
  advertisement creating, animoto used
      213-215
  cause and effect diagram recipe 121-126
  chain composition recipe 140, 141
  character, developing 64-67
  concluding sentences, writing 111, 112

Thank you for buying
Moodle 1.9 English Teacher's Cookbook

About Packt Publishing

Packt, pronounced 'packed', published its first book "*Mastering phpMyAdmin for Effective MySQL Management*" in April 2004 and subsequently continued to specialize in publishing highly focused books on specific technologies and solutions.

Our books and publications share the experiences of your fellow IT professionals in adapting and customizing today's systems, applications, and frameworks. Our solution based books give you the knowledge and power to customize the software and technologies you're using to get the job done. Packt books are more specific and less general than the IT books you have seen in the past. Our unique business model allows us to bring you more focused information, giving you more of what you need to know, and less of what you don't.

Packt is a modern, yet unique publishing company, which focuses on producing quality, cutting-edge books for communities of developers, administrators, and newbies alike. For more information, please visit our website: www.packtpub.com.

About Packt Open Source

In 2010, Packt launched two new brands, Packt Open Source and Packt Enterprise, in order to continue its focus on specialization. This book is part of the Packt Open Source brand, home to books published on software built around Open Source licences, and offering information to anybody from advanced developers to budding web designers. The Open Source brand also runs Packt's Open Source Royalty Scheme, by which Packt gives a royalty to each Open Source project about whose software a book is sold.

Writing for Packt

We welcome all inquiries from people who are interested in authoring. Book proposals should be sent to author@packtpub.com. If your book idea is still at an early stage and you would like to discuss it first before writing a formal book proposal, contact us; one of our commissioning editors will get in touch with you.

We're not just looking for published authors; if you have strong technical skills but no writing experience, our experienced editors can help you develop a writing career, or simply get some additional reward for your expertise.

Moodle 1.9 Teaching Techniques

ISBN: 978-1-849510-06-6   Paperback: 216 pages

Creative ways to build powerful and effective
online courses

1. Motivate students from all backgrounds,
   generations, and learning styles

2. When and how to apply the different learning
   solutions with workarounds, providing
   alternative solutions

3. Easy-to-follow, step-by-step instructions with
   screenshots and examples for Moodle's
   powerful features

4. Especially suitable for university and
   professional teachers

Moodle Administration

ISBN: 978-1-847195-62-3   Paperback: 376 pages

An administrator's guide to configuring, securing,
customizing, and extending Moodle

1. A complete guide for planning, installing,
   optimizing, customizing, and configuring Moodle

2. Secure, back up, and restore your VLE

3. Extending and networking Moodle

4. Detailed walkthroughs and expert advice on best
   practices

5. Checklist of over 100 common problems
   with solutions

Please check **www.PacktPub.com** for information on our titles